How to Get Married
After 35

How to Get Married
After 35

A Game Plan
for Love

Helena Hacker Rosenberg

with a foreword by Connell Cowan, Ph.D.,
coauthor of *Smart Women, Foolish Choices*

HarperPerennial
A Division of HarperCollinsPublishers

GRATEFUL ACKNOWLEDGMENT IS MADE TO THE FOLLOWING FOR PERMISSION TO REPRINT PREVIOUSLY PUBLISHED MATERIAL:

Alfred A. Knopf: Excerpt from *The Fall*, by Albert Camus. Translated from the French by Justin O'Brien. First American edition published by Knopf, New York. Copyright © 1956. Reprinted with permission of Alfred A. Knopf.

Alley Music Corp. and Trio Music Co., Inc.: Lyrics from "Ring Them Bells," by John Kander & Fred Ebb. Copyright © 1970. Reprinted with permission. All rights reserved.

Eleanor Harris (Howard): Excerpt from *The Real Story of Lucille Ball*, copyright © 1954. Originally excerpted in *Reader's Digest*. Reprinted by permission of the author.

Rosemary A. Thurber: Excerpt from "The Shore and the Sea," collected in *Further Fables for Our Time*, by James Thurber. Copyright © 1956 James Thurber. Copyright © 1984 Rosemary A. Thurber, published by Simon & Schuster. Reprinted with permission of Rosemary A. Thurber.

Simon & Schuster: Excerpts from *Necessary Losses: The Loves, Illusions, Dependencies, and Impossible Expectations That All of Us Have to Give Up in Order to Grow*, by Judith Viorst. Copyright © 1986 by Judith Viorst. Reprinted with permission of Simon & Schuster and Lescher & Lescher, Ltd.

Designed by Nancy Singer Olaguera

The Library of Congress has catalogued the hardcover edition as follows:

Rosenberg, Helena Hacker, 1948–
    How to get married after 35 : a game plan for love / Helena Hacker Rosenberg. — 1st ed.
        p.   cm.
    Includes bibliographical references.
    ISBN 0-06-017493-5
    1. Mate selection. 2. Marriage. 3. Middle aged women—Life skills guides.
I. Title.
HQ801.R695   1998
646.7'7—dc21   97–36024

ISBN 0-06-093033-0 (pbk.)

99 00 01 02 03 ❖/RRD 10 9 8 7 6 5 4 3 2 1

In memory of my beloved father,
Harold A. Shapiro

For Charlie, my anchor,
and Rebecca Clare, my light

"I don't know anything about luck. I've never banked on it, and I'm afraid of people who do. Luck to me is something else: hard work—and realizing what is an opportunity and what isn't."

—Lucille Ball, *The Real Story of Lucille Ball,* by Eleanor Harris (1954)

Contents

Foreword

Few desires in our lives are more compelling than the wish to find and bond with that special partner—our mate. But what prepares us for that precarious path to love? How do we avoid the mistakes we learned from our flawed models? How do we tone down unrealistic expectations so our experiences aren't a setup for heartache and disappointment? How do we move beyond the seductiveness of drama and excitement, trusting the value of calmer waters and a steadier pulse? How do we keep hope alive and value intact when those inevitable little doubts creep into our thoughts and dampen our belief in ourselves?

These dilemmas present hurdles to even the most hearty and fearless among us. But for the woman over 35, these challenges can be particularly daunting. This woman may already have felt the sting of love gone awry, causing her to pull back a bit, trusting less in herself or in the men she meets. Or this woman may have thrown her energies into the pursuit of educational or career goals, only now becoming aware of the jitters and pushy internal pressures caused by a ticking clock. She might have noticed that her expectations and thoughts of relationships have lost some of the flexibility and bounce they had in earlier days, that optimism and belief seem harder to hold on to. Or that her tolerance for discomfort has narrowed, and her reliance on the company of friends has increased. Or this woman may have lost a mate, and simply not know quite where and how to start over.

Whatever the reason, the woman over 35 has special needs in her search for love. For starters, she needs the encouragement to know it can be done, that the path to love does have markers along the way and she needn't blaze her own trail. She needs a guide who's done it successfully, someone who's drawn the blueprint, mapped out the hidden potholes, dead ends, and detours. The woman over 35 needs a plan for how best to look for a man, and how to recognize the one who won't be simply a good date, but a good fit. She needs to overcome any sense of being a victim, any clinging to tired excuses whose single purpose is to delay and avoid action. She needs to learn to overcome passivity, disbelief, and the seductive comfort of the familiar.

While there is much to commend about Helena Hacker Rosenberg's book, what I like best is her "feel" for the woman at midlife looking for love. Her sensitivity, her step-by-step, no-nonsense approach, could only have come from someone who *was* that woman, someone who had found her *own* way to a healthy, loving marriage. Hers is the wisdom of the trenches, gained through her own experiences as well as those of the many women she's helped. Searching for a mate can be a lonely, sometimes even an overwhelming process. But no one reading this book will feel alone; she will feel sheltered, understood, and always encouraged.

Don't think for a moment, though, that the book is simply easy. The approach is empathic without ever being coddling. I guess it's just human nature for all of us to hope we'll reach our goals and find happiness with ease and comfort. But we all know that growth, change, and new experiences are accompanied by making a stretch. And stretching can be uncomfortable.

The "stretch" you'll be asked to make will be illuminating. You'll reconnect and find value again in aspects of yourself that may have been lost or ignored. And you'll learn how to treasure that uniqueness and use it in your search for a mate. You'll be asked to take action, to make critical decisions, to turn flabby abstractions about love and relationships into realistic specifics. You'll be asked to give up notions about love that haven't worked for you, that probably don't work for anyone. And you'll be asked to honor and protect the best of you, and shown how necessary that protection is in finding the right man for you.

Read on. Take the adventure. Trust the process. Know that you, too, can be successful. The little stitches of discomfort along the way will be well worth it, richly rewarded.

—*Connell Cowan, Ph.D.*

Acknowledgments

Writing this book has been an honor and a delight, in no small measure because of the help and support of the special people whom I would like to thank at this time:

To Jeannette Multer, for believing I could write while I was still a schoolgirl with not much to say;

To Daniel Menaker, for encouraging me to think big and for lending his name in the service of my progress;

To my talented agent Lisa Bankoff at ICM, for first believing in this project and for never wavering in her faith; and to Lisa's assistant Abigail Rose, for her kind attention to my needs;

To my gifted editor Peternelle van Arsdale, for championing the book among her colleagues and for her always deft and sensitive editing of the manuscript;

To Fiona Hallowell, who adopted this book as her own, polished it with a sure hand, and guided it to publication;

To the wonderful folks who work in the Reference Department and Periodicals Room of the Beverly Hills Public Library, for their intrepid assistance and good humor;

To Tracey Alexander, Katherine Bouton, Judith Daniels, Janet Fireman, Judie Gregg Rosenman, Hella Hershson, and Lindsay Maracotta—dear friends all—for their time and input at various stages in this book's development. Their enthusiasm, honesty, and affection have meant the world to me;

To my dear friend Susan Weintraub, whose pesky prodding served me well and to whom I am immensely grateful;

To the many clients and friends who graciously shared their personal stories with me and without whom this book never could have been written;

To Rabbis Dov Heller and Joel Oseran and to Chana Rachel Schusterman, whose work inspires me and whose lives humble me;

To my brother David Shapiro, for giving me the rare gift of unconditional love and support, and for his continuing belief in my creative endeavors;

To my exceptional parents, Pauline Shapiro and the late Harold Shapiro, for reading every word of this manuscript and offering their loving constructive criticism, and for teaching me by their example that marriage to the right person can be a great unparalleled adventure;

And to my husband, Charlie, who agreed to be the de facto subject of this book without a clue how it would turn out, for his computer magic, his weekend baby-sitting, his patience, his boundless pride in my accomplishments, and his enduring friendship, commitment, and love.

Introduction

At age 44, I finally married the man of my choice, and in my wedding toast to my new husband, I summed up my feelings on the matter: I had always believed that someday my prince would come, but as the years went by, I had begun to worry whether he would arrive while I was still ambulatory.

My route to the altar had been an indirect one, filled with challenges and detours and even a certain degree of pain. For that reason, my arrival at my marital destination was especially sweet. Those who knew me well understood the historic import of these nuptials, exemplified by the response of one male friend when I phoned him with the wedding news: Of course he would be making the 3,000-mile trip for the celebration. He needed to witness what he called "this clear triumph of hope over experience." I knew, however, that while hope had been a necessary ingredient in my ultimate success, there had been forces at work that were far more concrete and quantifiable.

Early adulthood does not prepare us for the effort it takes to find and marry an appropriate mate later in life. When we are in our 20s and early 30s, we often believe that there exists an unlimited pool of eligible people from which to draw for dates and relationships. In reality, we meet more eligible people in our younger years not only because there *are* more eligible people, but also because our youthful lifestyles foster variety, spontaneity, and an openness to change.

By the time we've reached our mid-30s, however, our lives are less fluid and our options less plentiful. With more and more of those around us paired off, we may become increasingly dissatisfied with our single status and more eager than before to find a partner. We may even worry that marriage will never be in our future. Despite our desire to meet that special someone, as the years pass, we all too easily fall victim to habit and routine—the twin enemies of anyone seeking a mate in midlife. Drained by the revolving demands of work, family, and outside commitments, we often end up with little time or energy for meeting new people. Then, too, by this stage in our lives we have become more discriminating about the type of person we wish to marry, which means that fewer of the people we do meet actually appeal to us as potential mates. The romantic disappointments we've encountered along the way only serve to further dampen our faith in life's rich possibilities, causing us to retreat deeper into ourselves.

In the face of so many reasons for discouragement, is it any wonder that a vast population of singles beyond the age of 35 find themselves without partners, often not by choice? Clearly, these people confront unique and distinct challenges if they wish to marry. Consequently, they need to approach the idea of getting married in a fresh and creative way.

Fueled by my own hard-won marriage, I began studying at close range what separates the people who find and marry mates in midlife from those who wish to do so but somehow fail to reach the goal. And I found that in the overwhelming majority of successful cases, including my own, one of two conditions was present: either the person was operating outside his or her natural and usual comfort zone (a new experience), or the person had begun to view in a changed way someone already in his or her life (a new mind-set).

The emphasis in each case is on the new. And whether the match came about because of a new experience or because of a new mind-set, one factor was common to both: The successful candidate had effectively clarified what he or she needed in a mate. These people knew what they were looking for.

My own marital odyssey, coupled with the insights gleaned from the experiences of others, inspired me to package all that I had learned into a practical format that I could share. Working with private clients as a relationship coach, I now offer a concrete program to help mature singles maximize their opportunities for marriage. This book is an outgrowth of that program and that work. It is an in-depth, step-by-step guide to finding a mate in midlife—a guide backed up by the real-life experiences of many of those who have made their own successful journeys to the altar, despite prior setbacks and unfavorable odds.

The principles I want to share with you here apply equally to women and men. However, since women are more likely to seek the help that a book might offer—and more likely to believe it is up to them to find the right mate—I have designed this book with women in mind. The tenets apply equally to those wishing to marry for the first time and to those seeking to remarry after divorce or the death of a spouse. (I myself had a brief marriage when I was in my 20s.) And the fundamentals apply whether you are in your 30s and 40s and still wish to have children, or in your 50s and above and have childbearing issues behind you. The beauty of this book is that the principles and the approach remain the same for every woman, regardless of her age or her marital history. Your only task will be to pick and choose which of the book's many ideas best suit your particular needs.

In Part I, we'll explore how taking personal responsibility, focusing, clarifying, and listening contribute to finding a mate in midlife. Part II will help you define more clearly what you are looking for in a partner, spot Nowhere Men before they spot you, understand the contemporary pitfalls to personal happiness so that you can avoid them, and see the hidden dangers in seemingly benign personal relationships. Concrete strategies for finding a mate in midlife are outlined in Part III. In this section you'll learn not only where to go to find eligible men, but what attitudes to carry with you when you do, why your ideal mate may already be in your life, how to assess a new man for his marriage potential, and why viewing time as precious works to your advantage.

The finished product owes a great debt to the many clients who granted permission for me to use their personal stories to illustrate certain concepts and themes. In the interest of preserving the anonymity of these generous individuals, some names, facts, and descriptions have been altered. However, in all cases the spirit and intent of the original stories remain true to life.

The reader will also note that I occasionally cite sources from psychology, philosophy, and the Bible to explain or elaborate upon a particular point. I use these examples for the powerful imagery they evoke, not their literal interpretation or academic application. However, readers for whom such references may hold stricter connotation should feel quite at home with the material.

Marriage is not for everyone, nor is it a requirement for a meaningful life. Some people do fare better when they fly solo, and they should embrace their singleness without apology. But for the great majority of us, there exists a profound desire for a significant and lasting committed relationship. This yearning for intimacy and companionship can be especially strong as we approach our middle years, when holding hands with someone wonderful can bring more pleasure than seeking the latest thrill, and when we recognize that the future is upon us and that the time for making changes is now. It is for these women that I have written this book. I hope it inspires you and sustains you.

Part 1

You Get What You Need When You Focus and Clarify

1

"It's Your Life": Free Will vs. the '90s Victim Thing

"Alas, after a certain age every man is responsible for his face."

—Albert Camus,
The Fall

A new client, Erica, came to me recently in search of ways to improve her chances for marriage. A 46-year-old, never-married legal secretary, Erica was attractive and assertive and seemed very eager to tell me her story. All the more reason that I was taken by surprise when, after I asked her to tell me about her life, she replied that she had no life. It turned out that much of Erica's time and energy during her adult years had been expended on her parents, a well-to-do couple whose emotional hold on their grown daughter was excessive. As I got to know Erica, it became clear that the responsibility for her family situation rested as much with her as with her parents; while she complained bitterly about their controlling behaviors, she had done little to free herself from their clutches. Contrary to what she had told me on our initial meeting, she did have a life; she simply did not want to take credit for it. Yet, by refusing to be accountable, Erica was sabotaging her opportunities for pleasure and contentment.

Dire circumstances can force individuals to take charge of their lives in ways they never dreamed possible. A timid woman discovers upon the death of her husband that she has a knack for running her husband's business, and under her tutelage, the venture outdoes its prior sales records. A man whose courage has never been tested marshals superhuman strength and leads his condo neighbors to safety during a rampant electrical fire. Diagnosed with cancer, a passive young woman comes to know her own unexploited capacity to fight the good fight, and buys more time for herself because of it.

But these heroic measures are responses to extreme stimuli. It is less obvious how to tackle the pedestrian responsibilities of everyday life, when the challenges are not especially dramatic and the payoffs subtle or seemingly nonexistent. Nowhere is there a universally accepted instruction manual for correct living, which is why so many people wander reactively through life, without a plan or a point of view, and with no felt sense of their own power.

People inquiring about my services as a relationship coach sometimes display this reactive nature. When they ask what I am going to do for them, and I respond that I am going to help them do for themselves, these folks are perplexed. They were calling for "the answer," as though the key to life lay somewhere "out there." What they fail to comprehend is that the key to getting one's professional or personal needs met "out there" is first to take responsibility "in here." We all know that the answer lies within ourselves, and yet we're all hoping that something or someone will come along to do it for us. People have been looking for someone else to blame since the beginning of time. Indeed, our Creation stories, such as the story of Adam and Eve's exile from Eden, are really about responsibilities and the consequences of our actions, not sin.

Even the most conscientious among us can surrender personal responsibility, often without being aware of it. An example from my own life illustrates the point. When I first began my work as a relationship coach, I was unsure of the marketplace and where I would fit into it. To test my new business, I placed sample ads in local newspapers and magazines. The ad copy, which I had written in the third person, mentioned the name of the business—How to Get Married After 35—and some details about it, but did not identify me personally. Concise and clear, yes, but a bit cold.

I thought the ads were pulling quite well, until my mother, a loyal fan and constructive critic, pointed out that I was passing up business by not taking personal responsibility for my new enterprise. By omitting my name and a first-person appeal to prospective clients—in a venture founded on my own life experiences—I was not only hiding but also forfeiting a chance to connect with people in a more effective way. Once I changed the ads, and in essence went public with my story, the volume of my business doubled. It was my first entrepreneurial lesson in the benefits of being accountable.

Looking back on the roads I have traveled, I am struck by the direct relationship between my acceptance of responsibility for my own happiness and the rewards I have reaped. As a child growing up in a small town in Arkansas, I yearned for the big city, and vowed at a very early age—six or seven—to one day end up in New York. I had never been to New York, you understand, but from movies and picture books I had a vision of it as a sparkling and magical landscape in which I belonged, and some 15 years later, I made the image come to life by moving there.

As a high school student thirsting for adventure beyond the confines of my provincial world, I applied to be a foreign exchange student, amid the hoots and howls of the boys who were my friends and tormentors—the odds of actually being chosen were so grim that they could only chortle at my folly for revealing the scope of my dreams.

They lowered their voices a few notches when the letter of acceptance arrived from the American Field Service and the PA system in the cafeteria announced my imminent departure for a whole school year in France. (It was not just an adjustment for my male classmates, however, but for me as well, for while I had applied for this unique opportunity, I had not thought through the reality of being away from my family for 12 whole months!) The experience ended up being an incomparable opportunity from which I am still benefiting today.

Much later, after working in journalism in New York for some years, I wanted to make a switch to the entertainment business in Hollywood. Clueless about how to get started, I wrote a letter to a movie executive I had never met, a lady I'll call Ms. D., whose recent promotion I had read about in a press release. She had a background somewhat similar to mine, and I wanted to know how she had used it to arrive at her current pinnacle of success. In my letter, I congratulated Ms. D. on her recent promotion and asked if I could buy her a drink, indicating that I'd love some advice on how to turn my career in her direction.

It was an unqualified long shot, sending such a request

to a busy, high-powered stranger, but as my father would have said, it cost me only the price of a stamp. If she hadn't answered my note, I would have been right where I was before—in my cubbyhole at the newspaper, editing an article on Led Zeppelin and eating lunch from a brown paper bag. Fortunately for me, Ms. D. did answer, and because she had a genuine desire to mentor young women in her field, she ultimately opened the doors that led me to a job in Hollywood.

But the most profound consequence of my having taken personal responsibility for my life is evidenced by my marriage at age 44, after a good number of years of wanting a mate. The secret? During those years, I never ceased to view my personal life as my most important project in development, and I fought consistently the urge to blame the culture for my fate. Unlike so many of the single women I knew, I remained upbeat and physically fit; my singleness did not send me into a downward spiral of bitterness and cynicism.

I recognized then, as now, that this had been a *very conscious choice.* Not the comfortable choice, but the only one that would ever lead me where I wanted to go. So each and every day, instead of engaging in useless complaining, I focused on what I could do to best serve my marital goal. Work? You bet it was work! But what of enduring value do we ever achieve without effort?

It's Up to You

When I ask a new client how much time per week she spends thinking about her personal life, a typical response is "All the time" or "A lot." But to the follow-up question, "How much time per week do you spend doing something about it?," I generally hear, "Not much."

A case in point is an attractive, soft-spoken divorcée who came to me not long ago, seeking to alter some of the patterns that were contributing to her singleness. This woman, whom I'll call Shana, was involved in community activities, including a local chorus and various charitable organizations, and she was clear about what she wanted and needed in a mate. Yet while she dated periodically, she had a history of ending up with men who liked her more than she liked them. She longed for a relationship with true mutuality and knew she would not remarry until she found it.

While on the surface it might appear that Shana had been taking full charge of her personal life, closer examination revealed otherwise: Instead of consciously setting her sights on a particular candidate, she routinely left the "choosing" to the men. Having surrendered her authority in the selection process, she would then proceed to date a given prospect, hoping that if she saw enough of him she would learn to like him over time. While this approach has been known to work for some people, it clearly was not working for Shana.

What eventually came to light was that Shana's divorce had made her wary of forging another intimate relationship with a man. She had been avoiding involvement with men who truly interested her to protect herself from hurt. Once she understood why she ended up in lukewarm relationships with men, she vowed to take a more active role in selecting her companions. "I know now that what my grandmother always said is true," she told me recently. "Somewhere out there is a lid for my pot."

While Shana had passively allowed men to choose her, rather than actively participating in the selection process, she lost no time in altering her behavior once she became aware of its negative impact. For other clients, however, relinquishing responsibility expresses itself as a childlike desire to be coaxed and prodded into doing what is in their best interest. I have vivid memories of a particular 30-something woman whose behavior signaled a consistent wish to be coddled and led by the nose through life. She displayed keen enthusiasm for the recommendations that came out of our meetings, for example, but once outside my presence, she exhibited no commitment to implementing them. At one point she even joked that I was her conscience and that she needed me in her life 24 hours a day—a suggestion that unmasked how flimsy were her expectations of herself. I would like to say that this woman made great strides in her personal life, but this is not the case. She did not make much progress because she had no deeply felt desire to change.

A few years ago, when I watched a John Stossel ABC special, *The Blame Game: Are We a Nation of Victims?*, I was struck by Stossel's comparison of the ethics of American immigrants earlier in this century with the prevailing philosophy of Americans today. The immigrants came with only the shirts on their backs, says Stossel, and with their "self-reliance, the sense that they were responsible for their destiny," and with that, they built "the most successful, most prosperous society the world has ever seen."

Stossel paints a less attractive picture of human nature in the present, observing that if you cheat, steal, or murder, there is a ready explanation: You are a victim—of economic disparity, of society, of alcoholism, of bad parents. The name of the game, offers Stossel, is to pin the problem on someone or something else. The proliferation of television talk shows featuring practiced victims who parade their emotional wounds before an insatiable public is but one example of America's romance with the blame game.

The point was brought home to me by William Glasser, a

psychiatrist who once observed that while misery is a choice not a command, few people recognize it as such. Misery does not feel like a choice, he offers, because playing the victim serves some other purpose for the individual—it's an attention-getter, for example, or it allows one to feel righteous, or it helps one avoid scary or unpleasant situations.

I know a 40-year-old woman who, when I first met her several years ago, was choosing misery on a regular basis. She was a professional complainer, whose most consistent trait was to blame externals for everything wrong in her life. Her mouth was set in a permanent frown, and her conversation always contained the same litany of gripes: "All the eligible men around here are unreliable and immature, they only want younger women." "This town is isolating and promotes superficial values." "Married women have it made." "I'm never going to find a man."

While some of her observations were valid and her frustrations real, nothing about this woman's presentation was operating to her benefit. She began to see that her responses were coloring her outcomes, and over a period of a year or so, she set about to remove the edge from her own personality. How? First, she made a conscious decision to notice and emphasize the good in situations and in other people. Next, she made a commitment to do serious volunteer work, which shifted her focus away from herself and her own problems. Finally, she enlisted the help of her good friends, asking them to point out to her when she might be lapsing into her old negativity.

These measures took tremendous focus (the subject of the next chapter), but the results speak for themselves. She is now a pleasant person to be with, she looks and acts more relaxed and serene, and this improved package has elicited more dates and callbacks from men. Most important, this woman is now at peace within herself, because she is taking responsibility for her own happiness, and in the process, allowing her best self to come shining through.

Sadly, not everyone has the wisdom and courage to self-correct in this way. Among my clientele, the most tragic example of personal irresponsibility concerned Cindy, a 45-year-old woman who came to me in a state of intense agitation: She needed to get married by September 1, to someone with money, or else her ex-husband was going to take her children away.

It soon came to light that this woman had been receiving huge alimony and child support checks for the past five years, during which time she had continued to live the exact lifestyle to which she had become accustomed while married to her wealthy spouse. However, during those years of high living she had not planned for her own financial future by going back to school, learning a new job skill, or taking some other step that would prepare her for life outside the domain of a rich caretaker. Instead, she had clung to the Cinderella fantasy that another magic suitor would come along. No white knight had appeared, and now her ex was trying to gain primary custody of the children, on the grounds that Cindy was ill-equipped to provide for them.

It must be said up front that the ex-husband in this case was clearly a lowlife of gargantuan proportions. But it is also true that Cindy had squandered the resources that might have helped her to fight the man on his own slimy turf. Rather than taking responsibility and challenging herself to stand on her own, Cindy was looking for a man to bail her out of her current predicament. I offered that what she really needed was meaningful work and a chance at true independence, not another husband, and proceeded to suggest various creative ways for establishing a financial base.

But each idea met with resistance and accompanying excuses to explain why it would never work. For Cindy, the notion of herself as an independent creature simply didn't compute.

I later learned that this was actually her second ex-husband. Husband number one had retired from the Cindy scene when he realized that she wanted a meal ticket more than a marriage partner. By the time I met with Cindy, she was feeling resentful of all the men she had dated who did not wish to take on the responsibility of a high-maintenance wife and two children. She was angry at these men who loved their fancy cars more than they loved her—although she herself had chosen materialism as her primary value. Cindy did not find anyone to save her by the September deadline, and because of legal maneuverings and court delays, she is still knee-deep in custody issues.

While most women aren't as rudderless as Cindy, at one time or another we all can fall into the same trap. Women far more independent than she can unwittingly cast themselves in the role of victim, all the while believing they are models of self-reliance. Jeri, a dynamic woman in her late 40s, began seeing me to figure out why, since her divorce some years earlier, she had been unable to connect with any one particular man. Jeri had a variety of hobbies and interests, which she pursued avidly, and she had consciously pared down the demands of her career to have more free time for a personal life. Indeed, noting how she had organized her schedule, I admired how actively she was trying to increase her chances for meeting available men.

But what was not obvious from a superficial look at Jeri's lifestyle was that she was engaging in all this activity and tumult with the attitude of a victim. As I made various observations and suggestions about fresh ways to effect some changes, she invariably reminded me that she was not young, that she was fragile and had been hurt many times in the past, and that I should be "cautious" about what I advised.

I pointed out that our work together would be fruitful only if I could freely offer creative ways of thinking, behaving, and doing, and that it was *her* responsibility to select what might work best for her from the rich smorgasbord of possibilities. In our subsequent meetings, her charismatic persona always seemed at odds with this tiny interior voice of a wounded, weary child.

By the conclusion of our private workshop, she had begun to see that her veiled tactic of shifting responsibility from herself to a second party was possibly detrimental to her personal relationships. Perhaps her seeming strength, along with her subtle habit of passing the buck, was the reason men easily attached themselves to her but always ended up walking away. These insights made a profound impact on Jeri, and she took them to heart. She now carries with her a self-awareness that I am confident will begin to translate into more satisfying relationships with men.

Are You a Victor . . . or a Victim?

When Cassius in Shakespeare's *Julius Caesar* exclaims, "Men at some time are masters of their fates: The fault, dear Brutus, is not in our stars, but in ourselves . . ." he seems to be dismissing the role outside forces play in the lives of men. But, in reality, what happens to us in life is a blend of matters both within and beyond our control. And the more emphasis we place on those matters that we *can* influence, the more fulfilling our lives will be.

For example, if I am five feet, three inches tall and long to be a willowy five-nine, no amount of effort on my part is going to produce those extra six inches. But this limitation is not the whole story, because I can choose to wear high heels, or I can concentrate my attention on all the advantages of being petite. In other words, I can pick my response to the hand that life has dealt me. Doing so will not actually make me taller, but it will make me more content.

Similarly, while I cannot manufacture more money to live on, or create more unmarried men than already exist on the national census rolls, I can maximize my opportunities for financial and marital success by focusing on what I can control. I can look for a higher-paying job, for instance, or perhaps decide to bring more discipline and enthusiasm to my current one—thereby increasing the likelihood of a promotion. On the home front, I can resolve to spend fewer reclusive evenings alone in my apartment. I can join a quality dating service. Or I can commit to an exercise program at a socially active coed gym. I have options!

Have you ever wondered why some people have catastrophic things befall them and yet remain optimistic, while a bad hair day throws others into a clinical depression? This suggests that what differentiates victors from victims is not what happens to them but how they handle what happens to them— in essence, how they embrace or reject their options. A victor is not someone to whom bad things never happen, but merely someone who refuses to be defined by the negative.

A recent news story brought home this point to me. The subject of the piece was Zoey Koplowitz, a woman with multiple sclerosis, who has "run" in the 26-mile New York City Marathon every year for the past seven years. Known affectionately as "the woman who finishes last," Koplowitz crosses the finish line in the dead of night, some 20 hours after the start of the race and long after the other competitors have drifted off to sleep. She does it, says the athlete, leaning on her crutches, to celebrate the spirit within that does not allow her to quit. We all hit walls at certain points in our lives, she explains, those points at which we say, "That's it, I can't do it anymore." But, she continues, "I am here to say you can get beyond the wall and reach a place where you'll never again believe in the impossible."

By her words and deeds, Koplowitz would seem to be living out the biblical prescription from Deuteronomy— "Choose life, so that you may live." But if much of what happens to us in this world is beyond our control, exactly how is one expected to "choose life"?

Theologian Dov Heller insists that the true struggles of existence are not external but internal. Life is a battle, Heller says—not a battle between other people and me, or the world at large and me, but between me and me. The battle concerns choices and good decision-making, and Heller offers that as soon as we cop out and blame externals, we have lost the war. This lost war is often expressed by the words "I can't." What a person usually means by this is "I won't." Locating the cause of one's pain or loneliness means having to do something about it. It means having to work on one's self, and possibly to change—a terrifying prospect for many.

In his national bestseller, *The Seven Habits of Highly Effective People*, Stephen Covey demonstrates that highly successful people have "proactivity" as a primary trait; rather than blaming circumstances and outside conditions for their behavior, they view their behavior as self-generated, based on conscious decision-making and choice. It is this proactivity, says Covey, that translates into results in the outside world.

We've all seen the opposite at work in other people's lives, and possibly even in our own. We've all seen what a recipe for failure it is when people consistently see their ups and downs as having been done "to" them rather than "by" them. Let's say you have recently returned from an exotic vacation and would like to re-create in your own kitchen one of the dishes you tasted. The reactive individual might wish to accomplish the task but would characteristically place impediments in the way: "I don't have a recipe for that fish stew," for instance, or "It would take a bigger pot than I own," or "The spices were so unusual, I wouldn't know where to start." In other words, the reactive person looks for reasons not to achieve the goal. When people say "I don't know how" or "I wouldn't know what to do," the translation is "I don't want to take the time and energy to learn."

The proactive individual who is hankering for that exotic meal does not think in these terms at all but naturally gravitates toward resourceful solutions: browsing the cookbook section of a good bookstore to find a similar recipe; borrowing a pot from a friend or neighbor; consulting a spice vendor or the reference desk of the local library about the specifics of the flavoring used in the native region. The final product, while tasty, may not be an exact replica of the original dish, but satisfaction comes from taking the initiative and generating results.

A prime example of proactivity and the rewards of personal responsibility involved a dear friend of mine, then in her mid-40s. Some years ago, the two of us completed a lengthy, stressful work project, at which time we decided to treat ourselves to a no-frills trip to Italy.

Nancy had been in an eight-year, on-again-off-again relationship with a man who wouldn't commit. Though this was long before I had put up my shingle as a relationship coach, I was hardly shy about dispensing free advice. During one of our many girl-talks, I volunteered that some of her best years seemed to have been spent on this ambivalent, self-absorbed man (a reality that she had been pondering on her own). As she sat on a rock overlooking a Tuscan valley, Chianti bottle in hand, my friend made a proclamation to the valley below and to any villagers within earshot: When she got back to the States, she was going to sell her car—a vintage sports model that reminded her of her youth and was always breaking down—cut her voluminous mane of shoulder-length hair, and find a husband, not necessarily in that order.

True to her word, upon arrival on terra firma Nancy jettisoned the stagnant beau, sold the car, invested in a sassy short hairdo, and started dating with impunity—calling everyone in her Rolodex to announce that she was on the market. Less than one year later, she was married to the man with whom she just celebrated her eighth anniversary.

While my friend clearly had a bit of good luck on her side, she helped to create that luck. Her personal life would have remained in its unsatisfying rut had she not believed that her own actions counted—and had she not demonstrated a commitment to change. Nancy just as easily could have chosen to view her relationship with an unmarriageable man as inevitable, her lot in life, so to speak. She had already devoted her crucial childbearing years to this man. It took supreme courage to resolve to find something better, for in this act was an admission of perhaps having achieved less than her potential until now. But rather than stick with a doomed relationship for fear of what breaking it off might say about her past choices, she "chose life," and radically altered the quality of her own.

Easier Said Than Done?

Why is it that so many of us resist the idea that we have to work for a good relationship? Susan Schenkel, a clinical psychologist who specializes in issues related to women and achievement, believes factors in the culture inhibit women from taking responsibility for their lives. Taking responsibility means accepting the consequences of our actions, says Schenkel in her book *Giving Away Success*. Schenkel contends that women have been programmed to be pessimistic about their ability to influence events. This programming starts in childhood: While boys are pressured into mastering their fears, girls are frequently encouraged to give up if a task or an environment is too stressful.

Women also tend to view their successes as emanating from something other than their own ability—luck maybe, or the generosity of a mentor. Perhaps we have been trained to see taking credit for one's accomplishments as being arrogant or pushy. Ironically, the same women who minimize their strengths all too quickly blame themselves for anything that goes wrong in their lives.

That said, it would be a mistake to conclude that cultural conditioning dictates everything that happens to us. Whatever messages we may be getting from our culture, it's up to us to adapt for our own survival and happiness. For example, my generation of women was raised to believe that we would be supported and cared for by men via marriage, but new economic and social realities caused us to join the workforce by the millions. Becoming comfortable with the notion of ourselves as doers is, similarly, a process of learning as we go along.

Getting Started

Give Yourself Room to Fail

It is easier to begin to transform our lives if we first soothe our anxieties about confronting change. Fear of failure is one of the biggest impediments to meaningful change; it can prevent the best of us from taking the next step, whatever that might be. Therefore, it is important to give ourselves room to fail.

For example, if you are overweight and know that your appearance is holding you back socially, do not berate yourself if your new diet and exercise program takes time to kick in. You may commit to eating right and jogging hard only to find yourself slipping back into your old habits a few weeks down the line. That upsetting false start might actually strengthen your resolve to stick with the program next time. It can be liberating to discover that, by giving yourself the latitude to make mistakes, you can actually become more of a winner.

Stop Looking for Approval

The initial step toward conquering any fear of failure is to stop looking for approval from external authority figures—this common habit merely inhibits performance. Moreover, it guarantees limited success, because it draws its only strength from the whims and caprices of others. Instead, practice giving positive strokes to yourself, thus becoming in a sense your own praising parent; this is healthy and constructive. For example, if you've made the effort to look especially lovely before going to a singles event, tell yourself how great you look. *Believe* that you look great and know that this is objectively true whether or not men approach you that night or call you later on. For others to value us, we must first demonstrate that we are worthy of being valued.

Approach New Responsibilities and Challenges in Stages

While working to free yourself from the constraints of outside approval, approach new responsibilities and challenges in stages. If you have never been on an all-singles vacation or tour, and would like to try one, register for a three-day weekend, not the two-week package. Starting small, so to speak, will be less intimidating and perhaps inspire confidence for a more extensive commitment next time.

This mind-set was invaluable to me in starting my new business. My coaching activities now include meetings with private clients, group seminars, the writing of this book, and speaking engagements in front of various organizations. But had I plunged forward with all these challenges from day one, I would have been paralyzed by the magnitude of the task and would have positioned myself for certain failure; only by building one endeavor upon another—acquiring confidence and expertise along the way—was I able to gain command of each facet and thereby succeed at all of them.

Learn from Minor Setbacks

Many failures are the result of a lack of persistence rather than a lack of ability, giving the undisciplined an excuse to quit. Knowing this, it is important to frame individual defeats as merely that: temporary roadblocks. Rather than using minor setbacks as reasons to cop out, or to confirm our worst doubts about ourselves, these glitches can more productively be viewed as learning experiences. Anyone who has had a bad date, or a bad relationship, hopefully walked away from that experience with a few insights about how to do it better next time. The appropriate question is not "What did I lose here?" but "What did I learn? How can I use this information to my advantage?"

Few of the inventions that make contemporary life easier would have found their way to us had their creators given up at the first sign of trouble. Thomas Edison, for one, failed thousands of times before inventing the lightbulb. Asked by a colleague whether these constant failures made him lose heart, the scientist replied, "No, I'm not discouraged because I've found thousands of different ways the lamp doesn't work."

Applying the Edison analogy, if you join a dating service and find that it is not working for you, use the experience as an opportunity to evaluate better ways of reaching your goal, not as an excuse to retreat from the dating world. You might find out whether other dating services in your city have a more active roster of clients, for example, or you may feel that the glitch for you is a lack of self-confidence when dealing with strangers in social situations. In that case, your altered course might be to invest in a motivational seminar or a support group that tackles the specific issue standing in your way.

Practice Makes Almost Perfect

Practice and repetition help us acquire any skill, from driving a car to surfing the Internet. On the dating front, practice and repetition—what I jokingly call volume business—help to make individual social events less loaded, so that no one man, no one encounter, becomes a focal point on which to prematurely hang one's dreams. Imagine that you've just returned from a bad blind date, wishing you had stayed home and watched *ER* reruns instead. If you'd been looking forward to this blind date for weeks and had no other social plans looming on the horizon, chances are you'd be depressed by the evening's outcome. On the other hand, if the blind date had been just one of many social commitments you'd scheduled on your calendar that month, you could more easily keep your disappointment in perspective. You might even find a little note of humor in the current fiasco.

Take Risks

Most enticing of all arguments for overcoming our fears and becoming prime movers is that we gain nothing by avoiding risk. Staying ensconced at home instead of venturing outside may keep us safe from hurt, but it also keeps us single. Only by risking failure can we grow beyond our current boundaries. That is why Adam and Eve are sent out of the Garden of Eden with the instructions to "go forth" and "fear not." To flourish—and keep the human race alive— they are called upon to take risks. No matter how one views the Bible—as gospel or merely as symbolic literature—the message can be equally empowering.

Some 5,700 years later, the two directives "go forth" and "fear not" resonate as being wholly modern and applicable: Take action, witness your own efforts making a difference, and in so doing know you have helped to create your own good fortune.

2

Focus: What Separates the Haves from the Wannabes

A former colleague of mine is now a famous mega-producer in Hollywood. He owns several luxury homes and cars, and has been the subject of numerous profiles in national magazines. He commands vast sums for his professional services, is a frequent recipient of honors and awards, and can get to virtually anybody on the phone. Yet this walking embodiment of the American Dream was a lousy corporate executive because he could not "color within the lines," as they say. He was incapable of being a good company soldier, because he needed to give his imagination free rein, even if that meant breaking a few rules or thumbing his nose at convention—behaviors that got him into more than a little corporate hot water.

But today this renegade is a colossal success as an independent entrepreneur precisely because he has a distinct vision of the future and never takes his eye off the goal. He cares passionately about every last detail of every project he produces, and he is fearless in his pursuit of what he deems creatively correct. And because he sees a clear picture in his head that everything is possible, he never gives up. This attitude may drive those around him nuts, but he gets what he wants, and nine times out of ten, his instincts are right on the money. This man is not smarter, or better-looking, or better educated, or more polished than anyone else. He is simply more focused, and with that directedness he has built an entertainment empire.

Focus has applications for all of us, personally as well as professionally, no matter our level of endeavor. One needs focus to be a successful parent, to become a law firm partner, or to finish a marathon. Without some degree of concentration, it would be tough to pass college entrance exams, or to become proficient at a sport, or to carve out a meaningful work life.

Daily we are challenged to use our focusing skills, often without even being aware of it. An athlete who skips regular workouts soon finds that jogging is a chore rather than a pleasure; a violinist who misses a week of practice suffers the consequences of giving a poor performance; and a father who does not make time for his young child soon finds himself alienated from one of the most important people in his life.

Have you ever watched a group of preschoolers at play? If you have, you may have noticed a wide disparity in their levels of focus and concentration. While some children distract easily, susceptible to the least bit of outside stimuli or commotion, other children continue to direct singular attention to the task at hand—solving a puzzle, for example, or constructing a toy. For the latter group, intensity of purpose and unwavering dedication to the goal are what help them achieve it. They may not be any smarter than the children who distract easily, but their ability to tune out the irrelevant clatter of the world around them helps them to perform in smarter ways.

Using one's powers of attention effectively means focusing on necessary tasks without distraction, concentrating until a goal is reached—all without wasting unnecessary psychic energy in the process. How well we apply or abuse this important tool has a direct impact on the quality of our experiences.

Actor Jim Carrey tells a revealing story about focus. As a young comedian just starting out, he promised himself that, by Thanksgiving 1995, he would make $10 million as an actor. To seal this personal pact, he wrote out a check to himself, for "acting services rendered," in the amount of $10 million—a check he carried in his wallet during all the years of struggle and hard work.

Years later, on schedule with the commitment he had made to himself, Carrey was offered a $10 million deal to star in the sequel to *The Mask*. Carrey's father, a financial failure who shared his son's dreams for success and whom Carrey loved a lot, died shortly thereafter. The comedian, in an act of sentiment, buried the fantasy $10 million check in the casket with his dad. (Carrey's acting fees have more than doubled since then.)

It is impossible to weigh how much of Carrey's success was due to raw talent, excellent timing, and good luck, and how much was due to focused effort on his goal. But it is safe to say that, had he not imagined his own success—and had he not made this vision a consistent priority, backed up by action and hard work—he would have been far less likely to achieve his dream.

But while most of us would agree that focus plays a primary role in professional, artistic, or athletic achievement, we tend to resist the notion that focus might be a crucial ally in the sphere of romance. For some of us, it feels embarrassing and unseemly to put emphasis on an arena we innately believe should resolve itself naturally. Perhaps we believe that focusing on marriage as a goal makes us look foolish or, worse, makes us appear undesirable. After all, doesn't love just blossom spontaneously for the heroines of books and movies?

When one is 22, and the opportunities for romance are plentiful, perhaps focus plays a lesser role. However, by age 35, one's options have narrowed somewhat even as one's tastes have become more refined. With a limited pool of eligible men from which to choose, it is precisely the focused and highly directed among us whose marital desires have the highest probability of being fulfilled. In this sense, achieving one's romantic goals is no different from excelling at any other serious endeavor: Those who pay attention retain the best odds, while those who daydream, or who distract themselves by staying in dead-end relationships, or who channel their energies in other directions, are likely to remain on the romantic sidelines.

For a woman to focus on her personal life does not imply that she become a piranha, ready to strike at every available male, nor does it mean that she must adopt a cold and calculating approach to men. Such negative connotations clearly reflect an outmoded notion of female behavior that has little resonance for today's proactive woman. Furthermore, suggesting that a woman become more focused need not signify that now she must turn her life inside out. For one woman, heightened focus could mean taking active steps to join a dating service, answer personal ads, or hire a matchmaker. For another woman, the act of focusing might be more subtle and low key and involve merely telling others that she is interested in meeting eligible men. But whatever her level of activity, the focused woman tells *herself* that she wants to find a mate, and she proceeds to behave in ways consistent with her goal.

This simple truth was not lost on Molly, in her 30s, who determined that she would marry a talented and creative professional in her field—she just wasn't sure which one! Molly is a lovely, wholesome person and a loyal friend, but she is not glamorous or beautiful—in fact, she is quite earthy and unadorned. But what she lacks in pizzazz she makes up for in focus. She had a plan and she intended to make it work.

Subsequently, she met a prospect whom she decided was "it"—a man in his mid-40s who was a moderate success in business and who was a kind and jovial companion. But he came with baggage. As a divorced father and the custodial parent of several young children, he was wrapped up in family obligations. And because the children's mother was unstable, the family dynamics were somewhat chaotic and unpleasant—so much so that a number of women who had dated the father before Molly had finally given up. They resented how absorbed he was in the constantly unfolding dramas at home and how little emotional energy he had left over for outside relationships.

But Molly took the long view and patiently saw this man through the next five years—years in which his children gradually outgrew their neediness and during which Molly was able to insert her own homespun brand of calm and reason into the equation. Molly's unwavering devotion and focus on what was important eventually convinced this man—whose previous relationships had been with more showy women—that he should marry her.

In a delightful display of poetic justice, the marriage came on the heels of an unexpected windfall: Molly's guy hit it big in a business venture, and a man who had once earned merely a nice living was an overnight multimillionaire. This was just icing on the cake of their happiness, though, because the tough years in which Molly had stuck it out had permanently endeared her to him. In turn, he knew that Molly truly loved *him*. They have since become the parents of a beautiful child and enjoy a fulfilling life.

Visualize Your Future

My own romantic history exposes a pitiful lack of personal life focus during my 30s, though I was woefully oblivious of this problem at the time. This state of affairs is best symbolized by what should have been a breezy summer romance of mine that stretched into a three-year, live-in relationship. The young man in question was witty and charming and we had enormous "fun" together, but there were several troublesome pockets of incompatibility just beneath the surface. Nonetheless, dizzy from the romance of it all, I invited him to move in with me at summer's end.

Our decision to cohabit after knowing each other so briefly had sprung from the simple fact that his apartment lease was coming to an end and he needed a new place to live—in hindsight, a thoroughly ridiculous reason for two grown people to set up housekeeping together! But, since I was not leading with my head, the faulty logic failed to register.

It was only a matter of time before our incompatibilities began to show. While we cared about each other, had a lot in common, and shared a clear attraction, many of our goals and values clashed. And because we were fundamentally mismatched, investing additional time in the relationship was never going to improve the mix for either of us. He was a very good man, and thoroughly decent, but we were not good as a couple. Had I developed Molly's degree of focus—had I kept my eye on the long-range objective of finding a life partner, which I wanted—this relationship would have remained what it probably was intended to be: a great summer romance.

What Molly had at that juncture, and what I clearly did not have, was a distinct vision; that is, she had a sharp mental image of the life she desired. While Molly had consciously charted what she wanted, and what she was willing to give up to get it, I had been treading water and functioning under the mild delusion that I would remain 32 forever.

Addicted to Love

"All You Need Is Love," the Beatles told us, and herein lies the reason so many otherwise smart and effective women lose focus in their romantic lives. Launching into romantic liaisons without looking, these love addicts come off their highs later and often find that what they have to show for their tumble is a nasty bruise to the heart, and little else.

In a culture that promotes instant gratification as the desirable norm, and that gives the quieter virtues of fidelity, honor, and accountability such short shrift, it is little wonder that there exists a national fixation on idealized love. One friend of mine no doubt speaks for millions when she says that focusing on her personal life takes away the magic—finding the right mate, she contends, should require no effort or concentration, but should spring naturally from the well of human experience. Of course, what she's overlooking is that focus does not mean an end to romance at all; focus merely channels our romantic impulses in the most favorable direction.

My friend's free-wheeling philosophy may sound exciting—catering as it does to a taste for high drama and surprise—but the bottom line is that an overreliance on serendipity in matters of the heart robs the individual of power and leaves happiness to chance. What a waste!

A playful examination of the language of romantic love highlights how easily one can turn to mush once hooked by its seductive lure. The expression "falling in love," for example, indicates by definition a lack of direction and forethought, as if the person had not been watching the road and had suddenly fallen into a pit. In his book *Erotic Faith*, Robert Polhemus notes that "falling in love" also carries with it the sense of "slippage . . . a sliding away of sure ground . . . a loss of control," suggesting "the possibility of turbulence as well as absorbing experience." Likewise, the phrase "head over heels in love" denotes an extreme state that behavioral psychologist John Alan Lee categorizes aptly as "a form of madness."

From the *Kama Sutra* to the poems of Sappho, ancient literature confirms there has always been an audience for tales of high romance. And today we need look no further than the romance novel industry, which is fast approaching the $1 billion mark, to grasp how hungry we are for the literature of love. Featuring such titles as *The Flame and the Flower*, *Blades of Passion*, and *Moonstruck Madness*, romance novels can entice us to become virtual addicts of the genre. While the plots once played out against fantasy backdrops such as palaces and pirate ships, romance novels are now just as likely to be set in contemporary homes and offices and to echo our lives in certain other details—a bow perhaps to demographics: 50 percent of the readership, which is almost exclusively female, work outside the home.

But it is one thing to lose oneself in romantic fiction and quite another to lose oneself in fact. Falling passionately in love is indeed a heady and wonderful experience. Scientists have actually studied the physiological response to falling in love, a state that is often accompanied by physical sensations such as loss of appetite, breathlessness, and sleeplessness. A *Time* magazine article I read several years ago pointed out that the substances affecting the newly smitten are in fact chemical cousins of amphetamines. The article emphasized that when these chemical substances subside and the passion wanes, the relationship often fades as well.

For a relationship to endure, something deeper has to happen to extend the experience beyond this initial rush. The problem is that books and movies would have us believe that the dizzy passion we feel at first is what love really is and should be. When our relationships with real people don't necessarily mimic the tumult we see on screen or on the page, we can feel crashing disappointment.

Dr. Michael Liebowitz of the New York State Psychiatric Institute calls individuals hooked on sensation "attraction junkies." They crave the intoxication of "falling in love" so much that they move on as soon as the first rush of infatuation ebbs, never sticking around long enough to learn the art and pleasures of long-term loving.

A recent client of mine, Emily, falls into the category of bona fide attraction junkie. A pretty, gregarious sales representative, this 47-year-old single mother consulted me about how to enhance her marital prospects, and in a short time, it became obvious how she was standing in her own way. Emily described her father as an aloof workaholic who connected poorly with others. She, in turn, had spent much of her dating life in pursuit of the opposite—a storybook romance. Dominating her prerequisites in a potential mate were "someone adventurous and exciting, someone who adores me, someone capable of satisfying my need for fantasy."

In a constant quest for the ultimate romantic high, Emily typically jumped into relationships quickly, sleeping with men on the second or third date and allowing chemistry to dictate the proceedings. She had experienced a succession of such relationships, and each one eventually ended in disappointment. Having set up unrealistic expectations for round-the-clock, high-voltage excitement, she invariably found each candidate lacking. Indeed, over time, no one could meet such needs, for they were predicated on a drive for sensation with little regard for substance. At no time was she stopping to assess a man's worth independent of his ability to titillate. She was chasing a phantom lover.

While Emily claimed she wanted marriage, I sincerely doubted her conviction. Her need for constant exhilaration led her to ignore the quality of the man—his depth, his character. Emily's emphasis on excitement rather than fulfillment revealed that she was avoiding true intimacy and was actually afraid to settle down.

Casablanca, made in 1942 and still one of the most watched, rented, and studied movies of all time, captures the difficulty of converting dream love into real love. Ilsa Lund, the character portrayed by Ingrid Bergman, though romantically in love with Rick (Humphrey Bogart), is forced by circumstance to remain with her noble husband, Victor Laszlo, a man for whom she feels love and admiration but not grand passion.

I believe audiences respond so universally to this Oscar-winning classic because, on the one hand, the film acknowledges a wish for transcendent romantic fulfillment, while on the other hand, it affirms the everyday virtues of respect, honor, and commitment as being the true measure of enduring love. While we would have liked Ilsa to be able to run off with Rick, somehow we would have liked her less if she had. And the ending of the story implies that, had Ilsa stayed with Rick, she would have eventually grown to resent him for his complicity in keeping her there.

Taking the Long View

For many of us, the problems attendant to focus do not concern misplaced priorities but, rather, a lack of consistent attention to the priorities we already have. The net result—whether the goal is getting into good physical shape, learning a foreign language, or finding a mate—is that we do not pay enough single-minded attention to make measurable progress. So we are always on the verge, often using our lack of progress as an excuse to set aside the project altogether. Health clubs that design multiyear contracts for jazzed-up clients count on a high rate of fallout from folks who lose focus—this is the reason such clubs have constant membership drives while never really increasing attendance.

Yet learning to focus and stay focused is an acquirable skill. Clinical psychologist Susan Schenkel relates that in research where participants with low expectations for success were specifically instructed to give their complete and undivided attention to a task, "their performance improved considerably."

Setting Goals

Keep Track of Your Progress

Studies confirm that learning to monitor our own behavior can actually help to channel it in a positive direction. A common example of monitoring that leads to positive results is the counting of calories—an indispensable tool for the conscientious dieter. But the applications are endless. For instance, if you are shy and tend to avoid socializing in groups, simply counting how many times you forgo such encounters can be enough to increase your daring. Your opportunities for pleasure—and possible exposure to eligible men—can be enriched just by staying conscious of your own resistance. The process also works in the reverse. If you find yourself engaging in some unwanted behavior—nail biting, for example—you can actually decrease its frequency just by keeping close track of how often you indulge in it.

I am well aware of having kept a focusing "balance sheet" earlier in my professional life. Years ago, when I began working in corporate environments and was trying to get my sea legs, as it were, I found myself intimidated when called upon to speak in creative meetings. This phobia, the brainchild of insecure thinking—"What if my ideas aren't good enough?" "Will I look stupid?" "Can I get through this presentation without looking nervous?"—kept me from participating, even when I knew the answer or had an idea I was sure had merit.

Recognizing that this irrational behavior would ultimately hold me back, I concentrated on the fear in order to overcome it. First, I sought professional help from a public speaking coach—which was very useful. In conjunction with it, I began to force myself to speak during group office meetings, keeping a mental log of how many times I had contributed during any one session. The more I focused on pushing myself forward, the easier it became to do so. Keeping score allowed me to pat myself on the back for each successful "point," and the increased confidence made the meetings progressively easier to confront. A side benefit was that I became less worried about being "right" or "wrong" and more invested in my overall productivity and enjoyment. This improvement was not achieved overnight, but it was made possible over time because I never lost sight of the ultimate objective.

Make Lists

Once I awoke from the inattentive behaviors described earlier in this chapter, focus became my invaluable personal life friend as well. I became a consummate list-maker, attacking my marital campaign the way I would have approached the challenge of changing professions. Had the goal been work-related, my list might have included networking and seeking the advice of others already working in the new field of interest; attending classes or seminars in the arena; consulting the *Occupational Outlook Handbook* to determine the long-range economic forecast for the prospective field; and doing part-time or volunteer work in the new field to test my level of interest and commitment.

Instead, with the clear goal of finding a mate, my agenda was geared toward expanding my social network. I recognized that once my workday got under way, my personal life "homework" would invariably be nudged to paltry second position. So I made it a habit to focus on the needs of my personal life at the beginning of my business day.

Knowing that I wanted to do something every day in the service of my personal life, and committed to this as an inviolate rule (more about this in Chapter Nine), I would arrive at my office each day a few minutes early, settle in with my coffee and bagel, and proceed to make lists, phone calls, plans, and arrangements that might further my marital goal. This means my "call list" at work invariably began with personal calls—to a friend to follow up on her promise to introduce me to a particular man, to an organization advertising an intriguing lecture series, to a dating service for information about rates and clientele, and so forth.

Do Something Positive for Your Personal Life Every Day

Starting my day in this fashion not only assured me that my private life would stay on the front burner; it also gave me a sense of well-being that carried me through the stresses and demands of the next ten hours—I had done something positive on my own behalf, I was not married to my work, I was making personal life progress and need not feel sorry for myself or lapse into cynicism or depression.

Some may say that this degree of emphasis has the potential to backfire—that concentrating so directedly could have the opposite effect by promoting anxiety and obsessive behavior. But I have never found this to be the case. I suspect that those for whom this manner of focusing creates anxiety are people for whom many of life's challenges stir up unsettling emotions.

Ask for Help—Judiciously

When I advocated to a new client the necessity of keeping her marital goals always in mind—the need to prioritize and not drift into activities or relationships outside the goal—she mistakenly interpreted this to mean that she must announce her intentions to the world. You need not take out an advertisement in the *New York Times*! It matters little whether everyone knows marriage to be your priority, only that you know it to be so and that your decision-making and behavior consistently reflect this value.

That said, there are people with whom it will be valuable to share your priority: friends and acquaintances who can be sources of fix-ups; men you date who are not right for you but who could become important links to other eligible men; people you encounter regularly, such as your doctor, dentist, lawyer, clergyman, contractor, insurance agent, and hair stylist—all of whom have rosters of clients/patients/congregants, and each of whom can be playfully approached with the assignment of introducing you to quality men (more about this in Chapter Nine). But declaring yourself to everyone you encounter, from the bank teller to the filling station attendant, qualifies as definite overkill! You are determined, not desperate.

Concentrate on the Positive

To stay focused in positive ways, couch your desires in the affirmative. Lamenting everything that is currently wrong, or that could go wrong, for example, does little to ameliorate a situation. Alternatively, acknowledging what is already good, and what can be made better, allows one to plant seeds in fertile soil. Merely framing wishes in constructive terms is a big step toward fulfilling them.

Pretend that you live in the suburbs and that you recognize that your social life would expand considerably if you moved into the city. You might be tempted to say, "I hate being out in the middle of nowhere—the isolation of this place is making me depressed. . . . I have to get away from here." But this only announces what you do not want. A positive spin would take you further—you might say, for instance, "I want to move into town to have access to more cultural and social events," or "City life will be a refreshing change from suburban living and will increase my chances for meeting eligible men." Meanwhile, until you actually make your move into the city, be creative about finding fun things to do in the suburbs. Take advantage of the social and cultural events that *are* available. The more you describe your goal in positive terms, the greater the likelihood that you will reach it.

Don't Waver

Once you are clear and committed in your determination to meet and marry an appropriate mate, every subsequent decision or choice is weighed in light of that goal. Any opportunity, however tempting, that conflicts with the goal or attempts to distract you from it becomes a clear "pass." Suppose that, after you commit yourself to finding a worthy mate, you meet a lovely man through a dating service or perhaps at a church or synagogue. He's everything you had in mind—everything except that, as a divorced father with many financial obligations and a demanding work schedule, he articulates his own committed decision never to remarry.

The unfocused woman could easily disregard his admission, thinking that she can eventually change him, or convincing herself that she would be willing to date him on his terms. *The truly focused woman, however, does not play these mind games with herself. She takes the man at his word, assuming he means precisely what he says. As terrific as he may be, he is not terrific for her, because he is not what she needs.* The decision about becoming involved with him becomes a nondecision, because she can see that a romantic relationship with him, however casual or undemanding, would only delay her from reaching her own goal.

The focused woman knows herself well enough to understand that, by passing up this ostensible opportunity, she is actually opening more doors for herself. The qualifier here is that she "knows herself"—a vital and hard-won capability, and the subject of Chapter Three.

3

Clarity: If You Know What You're Looking For, It's Easier to Find

"All men should strive to learn before they die what they are running from, and to, and why."

—James Thurber, "The Shore and the Sea," *Further Fables for Our Time*

Maryanne, an attractive new client, came to me lamenting the fact that she was nearing 50 and was still alone. She had adult children, her own successful business, and an active social life. We discussed what she *wanted* in a mate and she indicated, somewhat apologetically, that money and status were very important to her. Her ex-husband had been only moderately successful in his work, and this had caused problems in their marriage.

Much later in the meeting, when she was feeling more relaxed and natural, and I asked what she *needed* in a man, she listed kindness, intelligence, warmth, humor, and understanding—none of which has anything to do with money and prestige. It turned out that Maryanne's mother was the one who was hooked on material things, and in her deepest self, Maryanne longed for a connectedness that money and status alone would not bring.

The distinction between needs and wants is a subtle but powerful one. Some people stumble in this area, because the things they think they want are often not what will ultimately make them happy, and they're so busy focusing on what they want, they can miss the things they actually need. The analogy I offer my clients who find themselves in this predicament is that of a woman walking through a desert, thirsty beyond reason, and completely unaware of the river at her feet.

How can we get in touch with this river? The only way to figure out what we need is to figure out who we are. The precept "Know thyself," which was inscribed on the temple of Apollo in ancient Greece, sounds deceptively simple. In fact, for many people, self-knowledge is the most difficult to acquire.

In the course of getting to know a client, I typically ask a host of questions, among them a request that the client verbally list five or six adjectives that describe herself. Surprisingly, a number of the women I meet are thoroughly stumped by this assignment, as though I were asking a question relating to advanced nuclear theory rather than to themselves. "Oh, jeez, I can't do this!" they may complain. Or they silently search the room, hoping to find clues about their own identities floating in thin air.

While some clients seem stymied by the question altogether, others answer readily, but with very little confidence:

"I think I'm smart," "I guess you could say I'm pretty," and so forth. Or, before answering the question, they might ask whether I wish to hear positive or negative traits. It often occurs to me that such clients are unaccustomed to thinking or saying nice things about themselves and reluctant to admit the things they don't particularly like.

When we lack clarity about our own natures, it is difficult if not impossible to determine what we really need in a man. Is it any wonder, therefore, that many women pass up good husband material without even being aware of it? Moreover, if we haven't discovered what is unique and valuable about ourselves, how can we expect others to appreciate who we are?

The Six Impediments to Clarity

Before we can accurately assess what we need in a man, we need to recognize the factors that might be clouding our sense of ourselves. There are six major roadblocks to clarity that I've witnessed in my life and my work, each with its own hazards.

Lack of Self-regard

To adequately assess oneself requires operating from a position of healthy self-respect. It is a classic vicious circle: If you do not feel worthy, you have little to give to others. We communicate our negative feelings about ourselves to potential mates, and, naturally, they respond accordingly. We assume the worst about ourselves and use other people as a way to reinforce our negative self-image.

One of the most common stories I hear concerns the letdown an insecure woman can experience as she mingles at a cocktail party. If she is talking with someone and that person moves on to chat with someone else, the insecure woman assumes that the other guest found her boring or stupid. She sees the other person's behavior as a measure of her own lack of worth and uses it as an excuse to withdraw. This, despite the fact that the purpose of a cocktail party is to mingle and circulate. In fact, it is the woman's own negative self-evaluation that is making her feel bad.

Imagine, for a moment, that things fizzle out between you and a man you dated for three or four months, whom you had begun to view as a potential mate. What is the healthy response to such a turn of events? While anger, disappointment, embarrassment, and even a brief spell of mourning might all be natural reactions, and we all will indulge in them now and again, at a certain point we have to pick ourselves up and move on. However, a woman with poor self-esteem might continue to see this ended relationship as a reflection of her own inadequacy.

Now imagine an alternate scenario, one reflecting a realistic and positive self-image. Instead of viewing the experience as a waste, we can ask ourselves important questions that will help us do better in the future: Was this man an appropriate choice in the first place? Did I adequately assess his character before starting a relationship with him? Were there signs of incompatibility early on? Did the two of us truly fulfill each other's needs, or were we both better suited to other mates—without this being a negative reflection on either of us? Such questions demonstrate a feeling of self-worth, because they show we can forgive ourselves as well as others and that we are committed to our own happiness.

Comparing Ourselves to Others and Expecting Rejection

Equally destructive to personal clarity is the unproductive but natural habit so many of us have of comparing ourselves to others. By measuring ourselves against another person's looks or accomplishments, we guarantee our own misery. There will always be someone else on the human food chain who has thinner thighs, a better job, a quicker wit, a bigger bank account.

I have often observed among my clients how unfulfilling life can be when we assume that others are far superior to us. The most common mistake for the woman who fears that others will find her lacking is to avoid social situations altogether. The reasoning seems to be: "Well, I may be alone but at least I'm not exposing myself to other people's criticism." However, while burrowing in at home is understandable if one is exhausted, short of cash, or simply in need of quiet time, when done on a daily basis it brings nothing new into one's life, except brief chitchat with the occasional pizza delivery man.

I often advise the single woman with no evening plans to try dining solo in a casual restaurant, which has the advantage of offering a nice meal, pleasant surroundings, and the potential for social interaction. When I suggest this little exercise, a sizable number of my clients express feelings ranging from discomfort to horror at the thought of occupying a restaurant table alone. People would stare, these reluctant clients assert. As one woman put it: "They would notice I'm alone and think I'm pathetic, and say to themselves, 'What's wrong with her that she is by herself?'" Another woman went so far as to say she would never eat alone in a restaurant because other diners would watch how she eats and evaluate her table etiquette.

In truth, most people are too caught up in themselves and their own concerns of the moment even to notice what is going on around them. And those who do make note of a solitary diner could just as easily interpret the table-for-one as being a positive choice—a busy, secure, independent person choosing to relax and unwind alone at the end of the day with a good book and a well-prepared meal served by someone else! Whether the experience is positive or negative is wholly in the mind of the single diner.

At the heart of all self-consciousness is a fear of rejection—a fear that we all have, and something that is among the most human of all emotions. I have a vivid memory of a beautiful and talented 30-something friend who reacted vehemently to my suggestion that she consider "playing the personals." "Oh, I could *never* do that," she exclaimed. "What if he didn't respond?" "What if he didn't?" was my reaction. "What difference would it make to your life?" My friend, a professional writer with a gift for language, had no real answer.

Of course, anyone seriously looking for a mate must accept rejection as part of the process. Indeed, rejection is part of life. Imagine for a moment a real estate agent or stockbroker who cannot tolerate rejection. He or she will never make a sale, because, as the saying goes, the road to yes is paved with scores of no's. Ultimately, you have to ask yourself which is more important—your wish to avoid temporary discomfort, or your desire to achieve long-term happiness. I hope you'll chose the latter.

Inflated Sense of Self

This is merely the flip side of impediment number one, a lack of self-regard. The same self-doubt that causes some of us to behave in a withdrawn, rejected way causes others to overcompensate for insecurities by acting arrogant and puffed up. Such excessive self-flattery can be just as unhealthy as excessive self-criticism, and can certainly blur one's personal clarity. To the outside world, we may appear to hold a lofty opinion of ourselves, but inside we feel small and insignificant.

A classic example of this tendency is the overachiever, the superwoman. Those of us who fall into the superwoman category secretly fear that no matter what we accomplish, we will remain inadequate and unacceptable. So we tend to seek out people who stroke our egos while we often pass up opportunities to know ourselves better or let others perceive our vulnerabilities. Since we invest so much energy in preserving the illusion of our superiority, we have little chance of cultivating self-knowledge.

Katherine, a client fitting this description, came to me on the rebound from a very painful romantic breakup. A successful executive whose self-definition revolved around her many accomplishments and awards, she had been in a long-term relationship with a man she had hoped to marry. Suddenly, and seemingly without warning, he had begun exhibiting behavior that objectively pegged him as being a man of poor character.

Katherine could not believe that a person she had trusted for so long had turned out to be so unworthy. Rather than look at her judgment in choosing him, however, she used this revelation to further bolster her perception of herself as a superior person. In fact, this man's fundamental character had not changed at all; Katherine had probably been misjudging him from the start, just as she had been locked into an ultraflattering vision of herself no matter what the circumstance.

If Katherine's experience reminds you of episodes from your own life, investigate how self-inflation might be interfering with your own happiness. To get started, ask yourself some leading questions. For example, do you have a hard time owning up to your errors in judgment? Do you *need* to be right even when you suspect that you aren't? Are you open to constructive criticism, or does even the gentlest criticism get your dander up? Do you let others know the real you, flaws and all, or do you work hard to conceal your vulnerabilities? If you suspect that you're prone to some of these behaviors, merely becoming conscious of them can begin to raise your level of personal clarity. The less you fall into the trap of self-flattery, the more content and approachable you will be.

Denial

Some 50 years ago, Rollo May, one of this century's leading psychoanalysts, wrote in *Man's Search for Himself* that not only do people "not know what they want; they often do not have any clear idea of what they feel." And herein sits the fourth stumbling block to personal clarity: denying one's authentic feelings instead of experiencing them. People sometimes suppress their unwanted emotions in an attempt to get rid of them, often because they are ashamed of having them.

I know a delightful single woman whose fear of feeling her true emotions once colored all her interactions. Marcia comes from a fairly large family, and her role in the family hierarchy had always been that of the easygoing, undemanding sibling. Marcia's brothers and sisters, on the other hand, have dominant, needy personalities: One suffers from chronic health problems and used to expect Marcia to be on call for daily practical help; another sibling has a history of debt because of bad business decisions and looked to Marcia as a ready meal ticket; a third sibling is always on the verge of another divorce and used Marcia as a free therapist; and so forth. Marcia, the stable solid rock, secretly resented the burdens she assumed but would not permit herself to express these negative feelings. This denial left Marcia in a helpless state. When Marcia's unexpressed anger started affecting her own physical well-being, she sought professional help.

Soon she began distancing herself from the demands of her family, and as she did so, her own health improved. The benefit to her social life was profound: Better able to locate and express her own needs, Marcia began to have more satisfying relationships with men.

Always Obeying "Musts" and "Shoulds"

To begin experiencing our real feelings requires that we remove a fifth impediment to personal clarity: the "musts" and "shoulds" that so easily creep into our vocabulary and can end up driving our behavior. Marcia, in the example above, was certainly influenced by these restrictive commands.

Defining our lives in terms of "musts" and "shoulds" means we end up living according to images of what we think others expect us to be.

One client of mine, Jenny, used the demands of single motherhood as the reason she had never remarried. Raising a daughter by herself left her no time to pursue an intimate relationship with a man, she told me. Not until Jenny's daughter went off to college did she begin to confront the hole in her own social life. While the stresses of single parenthood cannot be minimized, it is also true that many single mothers do remarry. So the issue for Jenny may have been less about her limited time and energy and more about her unwillingness to carve out personal time, separate from the needs of others. In Jenny's case, too, her mothering "musts" and "shoulds" became an excuse for avoiding the disappointments of the dating world. By blaming her family situation for her singleness, she did not have to take emotional risks.

Doing Too Much, Reflecting Too Little

Finally, personal clarity thrives most readily when one is in a mode of *being* rather than *doing*. The Judeo-Christian ritual observance of a day of rest, the Sabbath, recognizes the need for space in which to reflect on the week's labors and to prepare for the week ahead. But our lifestyles today rarely foster such enforced contemplation. It is hard to know our own priorities—what's valuable, what's expendable—when we allow ourselves no time for reflection. We easily get caught up in meaningless activity, with people who don't matter much to us. When this happens, we don't necessarily make the best decisions, including the best decisions about men.

When I left the corporate world and pared down my lifestyle, I did so precisely to allow myself more breathing room and more time to chart a personal life. As I became less frenetic, I got more in touch with the essential ingredients of my own happiness and the fundamental values I was looking for in a mate. These were not new values for me, but my connection to them had been blunted by too much motion and too little introspection.

Of course, what frightens many of us about slowing down is that, without escapist activity to distract us, we will be forced to look inward. However, only when we take the plunge and have the courage to be alone with ourselves can the Delphic edict "Know thyself" truly be fulfilled.

Setting Goals

Now that you have a better sense of who you are and what might be holding you back—lack of self-regard; comparing yourself to others and expecting rejection; an inflated sense of self; denial; always obeying "musts" and "shoulds"; and doing too much, reflecting too little—what other tools can enhance your experience of self-knowledge? First, set realistic, achievable goals. This does not mean compromising your standards. It requires, however, that the standards be formed with an open mind and a flexible outlook, because narrowing one's sights excessively is tantamount to having no sights at all.

An out-of-work executive who keeps turning down job offers because they are beneath him would do well to reassess his benchmark. A child learning to shoot baskets who constantly compares himself unfavorably to an agile older brother will naturally undermine his own progress. And a woman of 40 who wants to get married, but whose laundry list of spousal "musts" excludes most of the human race, may find herself without the love she needs. When a client displays this brand of perfectionism, I fear she is less open to commitment than she realizes.

In *Perfect Women,* author Colette Dowling describes the familiar syndrome of women who want partners and yet "price themselves out of the market . . . in the search for a star to fall in love with." In other words, they are so rigid about what they consider an appropriate choice that no one measures up. Dowling pinpoints the root of this thinking as a fear of intimacy: The woman, frightened to actually put herself in the vulnerable position of loving and being loved, constructs an aloof defense, which translates into "You're not good enough for me." So the need for a perfect lover is tied into a profound feeling of inferiority. These women are looking for a man to buttress their own devalued sense of self.

Women who fall into this category end up focusing on the most superficial, and alterable, aspects of a man's demeanor—his manner of dressing, for example, or the way he cuts his hair—rather than on the values he stands for or the quality of his character. Such women quickly reject candidates on the basis of these superficial imperatives. And since no one can meet their stringent standards, they eventually convince themselves that there are no good men out there. They keep themselves at a distance, sabotaging their chances for happiness by rejecting worthy but flawed men and pursuing only the elusive, unattainable ones.

Renee, the lovely sister of a friend of mine, is just such a woman. Like Maryanne, whose mistaken obsession with money and status opened this chapter, Renee has long been drawn to men of power and position. Time and again, she has been disappointed in love by these high-profile, high-flying types; yet she remains blind to the notion that a more down-to-earth guy might be a reasonable alternative. A bright, kind, gainfully employed man is not sufficient for her. He must be outsized, a little more than mortal.

It is noteworthy that this same woman admires and appreciates the basic, wholesome, accessible, "good" men to whom some of her friends are married. But she discounts such men as suitable partners for herself—even when well-intentioned friends try to point her in that direction. Meanwhile, she remains lonely despite an interesting job in the public eye and an active social life; she longs for a companion with whom to share her mature years but clings to requirements no one can meet.

Clearly, this is not what you want, or you wouldn't be reading this book. There is an alternative to pricing oneself out of the market, and that is to realistically prioritize one's requirements of a potential mate. First, determine the categories that you deem to be deal-breakers—and unless you are an absolute wimp, you will have a list of legitimate prerequisites. Perhaps you are committed to your faith and want a man who shares your religious beliefs. Or you are highly independent and want a man who is not threatened by your style. These become your unalterable needs. In my own case, my nonnegotiable requirements in a man included shared values, education, good chemistry, kindness, common religion, optimism, and a willingness to start a family.

Next, isolate what factors you can be flexible on—and if you truly want to marry, this list had better be as long or longer than the first list! Be honest and list only those areas on which you can be more open-minded without feeling resentment down the line. For me, the negotiable areas included a flexible attitude about relocating, children from a prior marriage, age, political leanings (as long as not extreme on either end), divergent interests (as long as we had a few in common), looks (as long as not a troll), and degree of affluence (as long as solvent).

Many women trying to list their requirements in a mate ask me how best to approach the task of separating deal-breakers from deal-optionals. How do we figure out what we can live with and what we can't? What if we meet a man and fall in love but find he lacks two of the prerequisites on our deal-breaker list? Does this mean the relationship is doomed to fail?

First, you must distinguish between preferences and needs, and between character and more superficial issues. A preference is something we'd like to have. A need is something we must have to be fulfilled. For example, I'd like to have a mate who is physically active, but I must have a mate whom I can trust. Never compromise on the essential qualities in a man that speak to such attributes as kindness, stability, generosity, honesty, and fidelity. These profound aspects of character cannot be changed, and if he falls short in areas that are central to your happiness, it will probably come back to haunt you. However, if you've been flexible on some of the more superficial issues—money, looks, or what have you—and if the man has other great attributes that off-set what you've given up, then chances are good that you'll be content. As with any important list-making, review your selections periodically to confirm that your original choices reflect your core values and needs.

An accurate appraisal of what you will and won't accept in a potential mate brings you that much closer to finding your special man. Once your parameters have been estab-lished, you can meet and interact with new men without dis-counting potential candidates or wasting time on obvious mismatches.

Perception Is Key

Now that we've discussed who you are and what you're look-ing for, let's examine what you're projecting to others. On this subject, I'm reminded of a man I know who can walk into a business meeting, make a long-winded presentation of a clichéd project—overstaying his welcome—and walk out believing he was a big hit. The rose-colored glasses that he wears prevent him from seeing how he is actually coming off. This explains why he's routinely shocked if he learns that a particular meeting was, in fact, a bust.

Such an astonishing lack of perception places one at a competitive disadvantage. While *defining* ourselves by the reactions of others is clearly unhealthy, having objective clarity about how we are being *perceived* in a given situation gives us power. An accurate reading of how we are coming across arms us with maximum data, thus allowing us to operate at full throttle.

A few months ago, I went to a wedding dinner at which the single woman to my right—objectively nice-looking and well groomed—ranted and railed against the type of men she was meeting, whose bad behavior she could not abide. The harangue built over mushroom soup, swelled with the Dover sole, and crescendoed on cue when the happy couple cut the cake. It was clear why men went out with this woman only once and never called back. She hated them!

For this woman—and for anyone to whom things keep happening in the same bad ways—the most constructive suggestion is a long look in the mirror. On the romantic front, for example, when global conclusions about the deficiencies of "all men" begin to dominate one's speech, it's time to remove the blinders and question how one's attitude and approach may be poisoning the stew.

If you suspect that you have this tendency toward blanket criticism of the entire male population—or if you view being single as a permanent, unalterable condition—start applying some of the focusing techniques discussed in an earlier chapter. Keep a written record of each instance in which you find yourself speaking in such broad, negative generalities. Next to each entry, write the date on which you said it. You'll be surprised how these offenses add up, and becoming aware of them is the first step toward correcting the problem. In concert with your record-keeping, assess how such unproductive carping may be a convenient excuse for not making positive efforts in your personal life. Review the six impediments to personal clarity outlined earlier in this chapter. Is your complaining perhaps a substitute for working to repair the deeper issues standing in the way of your happiness?

In the years I've been coaching women and men who yearn for the companionship of a mate, I am still occasionally struck by how little effort they seem to have expended to make themselves truly companionable. By this I mean that they expect to attract quality partners without cultivating the social graces, range of interests, sensitivity, and self-perception that might pull such people into their orbits.

One does not need to be beautiful, rich, or multitalented to be a "good catch." But women who tap every asset at their disposal and make the most of their natural attributes—physical, spiritual, emotional, and intellectual—easily outdistance women who complain and do nothing. Infamous courtesans such as Louis XV's mistress Madame du Barry or influential spouses such as Napoleon's Empress Josephine ascended into the royal sphere not by sex alone but by honing their social skills. They worked at becoming well-versed, empathic, convivial partners, thus making them indispensable to their men. These women understood the art of what psychologist Toni Grant in *On Being a Woman* calls being "a muse to man"—a companion who inspires rather than diminishes the opposite sex.

There is nothing inspirational about a charmless, harsh woman who labels all men as deficient. Conversely, there is little to recommend a passive, unsmiling woman who waits on the sidelines for men to entertain her, rather than pursuing interests that could make her a spirited conversationalist in her own right. A woman who tends toward one of these extremes may well find herself at a romantic impasse until she works to change the balance. In some cases, professional help may be needed to correct the intimacy problems that prevent her from moving forward. This help can take the form of private sessions with a trained psychologist or counselor, or relationship seminars led by trained professionals.

Our ability to perceive accurately how others are viewing us extends to the physical as well. Indeed, physical appearance—especially weight and grooming habits—directly influences our successes and failures on the dating front. My generation, coming of age during the Women's Movement, was particularly afflicted by propaganda claiming that physical appearance was irrelevant—we should be appreciated for ourselves, without reference to superficial concerns. To focus on the physical was beneath us, we were told.

It can now be stated with no fear of political reprisal: Men respond to visuals! Any woman seeking to capture a good job or a good man must accept this fact. Instead of lamenting this state of affairs, the smart woman needs to work with it. While it would be wonderful to be appreciated only for one's mind and inner beauty, men do not generally look deeper unless the exterior catches their attention. So packaging does count!

Therefore, make an honest appraisal of your physical presentation and commit to improving it where possible. If you are overweight, stop pretending and do something about it. (More about this in Chapter Seven.) If you have little flair for fashion, get some professional advice about developing a personal style. Or, if that is not within your budget, study fashion magazines with an eye toward elevating your fashion sense. If you stick with simple, classic choices, you can't go wrong. This is especially important to remember if your clothing budget is limited and must accommodate many social situations. Whatever you do to enhance your manner of dressing, make certain that your choices suit you. A skintight minidress and exaggerated, platform mules may be charming on a hard-bodied 22-year-old, but such attire looks inappropriate on a 43-year-old businesswoman. After all, you want to appear contemporary and fashionable, not foolish.

One advantage of being over 35 is that we can relish our womanly good looks and play to them. This does not mean we must refrain from creating a sexy and alluring presence, but we should be enticing in the subtle manner of a seasoned adult, not the obvious excesses of a kewpie doll. We are grown-ups and want to be perceived that way. A few pointers: Invest in a good haircut and any product that can take away the gray without making you look as though you just stuck your head in a can of paint. (Keep in mind that a lighter hair color will also lighten your looks, so consider some well-placed highlights rather than a drastic change.) Remember that a healthy, fit appearance is always attractive. Rather than applying more makeup or buying flashier clothes—two of the biggest grooming mistakes we can make in an attempt to look younger—let your natural self shine through. Invest in periodic facials to keep your skin clear and healthy, take care of your teeth, and, yes, exercise. And by all means avoid overpowering fragrances. There is no surer way to announce one's age than to use a heavy hand with scents and cosmetics. Easy does it.

The road to self-knowledge and accurate self-perception is a challenging one. Being honest with ourselves can be a painful proposition, and it is tempting to want to just get by, rather than actually get clear. Furthermore, though our ways of thinking and behaving often may be counterproductive, they have been in place for a long time and are not always easy to modify. Of course, the danger in not striving for sharp personal clarity is that we end up living partially in the dark. To attain the fulfillment of a committed intimate relationship, we must first seek the light by reaching for the truth about ourselves.

Accepting Yourself

The strategies addressed in this book so far—accepting personal responsibility, learning to focus, mastering personal clarity—succeed best when informed by self-acceptance. How does self-acceptance reveal itself in practical terms? Self-acceptance means liking yourself despite your flaws. It means knowing there is room for improvement while believing that you're worth it. To be self-accepting is to know how to soothe yourself and be the source of your own comfort. To be able to spend periodic time alone without feeling lonely or restless. To know how to derive pleasure in the moment—what theologian Dov Heller calls "pleasure bursts." It does not mean giving up on the desire for a loving marriage partner—far from it! But it does mean appreciating and celebrating the life you currently have while you are actively engaged in the serious business of finding a mate. And rejoicing in the moment has the added benefit of making you a more appealing person, since you thereby project optimism, not desperation.

Psychologist Melvyn Kinder, in his book *Going Nowhere Fast*, offers that self-acceptance requires relinquishing the impossible demands of the "Perfect Self." In Kinder's view, healthy self-acceptance comes only after we have learned to tolerate all the parts of ourselves—even the parts we do not particularly like.

Embracing the whole, warts and all, allows us to go forward in a positive spirit. My thighs may be too big, my oversensitivity to criticism may need vigilant monitoring, I may be abrupt with coworkers from time to time and immediately regret it. But none of this makes me a bad person, just a person who quite naturally makes mistakes. The curious thing about self-acceptance is that when we stop being overly harsh on ourselves, we end up being more tolerant of others as well. This has a direct bearing on our chances of finding a mate, for the polished edges make us softer and more empathic and strengthen our capacity to love.

But self-acceptance cannot be achieved overnight. Getting to this state of grace is an evolutionary process. There will *always* be certain people with whom we do not connect. Not everyone will be to your liking, nor you to theirs. Therefore, you should expect not to connect some of the time and view such occurrences as a part of life, not as failures. There is too much diversity in the world for it to be otherwise. And how vanilla life would be if these colors and shadings were not part of its fabric! But for every person out there with whom you do not mesh, there will be others with whom you do. And the best way to connect with these people—friends of both sexes as well as prospective mates—is to risk letting your real, unedited self be known.

The Reality Check

To test how you rate in the arena of personal clarity, complete the mini reality check outlined below. Using a separate piece of paper, enter numbers 1 to 12, then respond to the following multiple choice questions by selecting (a), (b), or (c) as your answer.

1: When you're on a date with a new man who spends the whole evening talking about himself, without asking any questions about you, do you (a) berate yourself for not being interesting enough to merit his attention; (b) throw your napkin in his face, walk away from the dinner table in disgust, and hail a cab; or (c) remain civil but assume he's very self-centered and not a great marital prospect?

2: When it comes to diet, exercise, and pampering yourself, do you (a) eat like a bird in public and a horse in private, bite your nails, and only *talk* about going to the gym; (b) hog the treadmill for hours at a time, count every last calorie, and talk only about current beauty fads; or (c) stay fit and content by eating and exercising in moderation, as well as treating yourself to regular manicures and an occasional massage?

3: The weekend is coming up and you don't have any plans. Do you (a) put on your ratty robe and fuzzy slippers and retreat into a familiar reclusive pattern as a way of avoiding social interaction and the anxieties it provokes; (b) call everyone in your Rolodex and make back-to-back plans so that you do not have to be alone with yourself for even one hour; or (c) make some plans so that you can widen your social net and be in the company of others, but keep a portion of the weekend free for private time?

4: You've been divorced since your children were small and you'd like to get remarried but (a) the demands of being a mother to a 20-year-old and a 22-year-old allow you no time for a life of your own; (b) there are no good men left on the planet; or (c) you haven't met the right man yet but you feel optimistic.

5: The five-year relationship you were in has just ended and you'd like to get back into the social swing, but (a) no one ever invites you anywhere or extends hospitality to you; (b) you're afraid you'll get hurt again; (c) you need a little time to mourn and regroup before returning to the dating circuit.

6: Your best friend's husband has set you up on a blind date with his old college roommate, a successful professional with a thriving business and a distinct desire to get married. When you open your front door to greet this marital prospect, you discover that he has ears the size of Texas and a haircut that would make a mother cry. Do you (a) refuse to be seen in public with him and slam the door in his face; (b) politely complete the date, all the while telling yourself that you could never ever consider marrying a man who looks like this; or (c) look beyond the superficial and accept a second date, realizing that this man may be terrific in a lot of other ways?

7: The message on the outgoing message tape of your home answering machine (a) is cold and brief and could be mistaken for a business phone message; (b) was recorded by your children and could make the caller feel he had misdialed; or (c) is warm and feminine and puts a stranger at ease.

8: In your personal and professional relationships, do you (a) find yourself ending up on the "short end of the stick," always giving more than you are getting back; (b) only feel appreciated when you're making other people jump through hoops for you; or (c) generally feel there's a natural give-and-take?

9: You're in a meeting at the office with your new supervisor and other employees who are senior to you. The supervisor asks a detailed question for which you know the answer. Do you (a) keep silent, fearing you may not know the answer after all; (b) wave your hand in the air wildly and smugly blurt out the answer; or (c) calmly answer the question, then silently pat yourself on the back for a job well done?

10: When a respected friend or coworker offers you loving, constructive criticism, do you (a) experience the criticism as a reflection of your innate worthlessness as a person; (b) become defensively incensed that anyone would dare to hurt you this way; or (c) listen with an open mind and benefit from the input?

11: You've just discovered that your favorite radio talk-show host will be speaking at a local venue this very night. You have no other plans, and it's too late to call a friend to join you. Do you (a) stay home and lament the fact that you had to miss the event; (b) go to the event but feel deprived that you are by yourself; or (c) go to the event, meet a few new people, and feel proud that you took advantage of this social opportunity?

12: While taking golf lessons at a public course, you meet a very good-looking, twice-married and divorced professional with four children, a bias against marriage, and a clear desire not to have more kids. You're a never-married 41-year-old who wants marriage and a family. Do you (a) begin dating him anyway, believing he might someday come around to your way of thinking; (b) give him the brushoff, since he's obviously a jerk; or (c) refuse to date him because he's not what you're looking for in a mate, but keep him in your life as a friend and potential source of introductions to other men?

Reading Your Answers

It is fairly obvious that choice (c) represents the healthiest response to these questions. If you responded with a lot of (c) answers, you no doubt enjoy healthy self-regard, an openness to change, and a willingness to take some emotional risks.

If you more naturally gravitated toward choice (a) when responding, you may need to do some work on issues relating to self-esteem, self-control, and accepting responsibility for your own happiness. The behaviors described by the (a) choices are ones we've all experienced in one form or another, but they are behaviors that hold us back rather than behaviors that promote personal growth.

The (b) choices reflect overly critical behaviors that express themselves as intolerance, closed-mindedness, and even arrogance. We have all been guilty of these as well, but if you found that the (b) choices most accurately captured your true feelings, you will want to take a closer look at how your rigidity is getting in the way of fulfillment.

Do not be too harsh with yourself if you could not answer (c) every time. Few of us could. This chapter is intended to suggest your level of personal clarity. After you have finished reading this book and begun to put some of its ideas into practice, retake the test and I guarantee you will find more (c) answers on the page.

4

A Man Tells You All You Need to Know in the First 15 Minutes . . . But Who's Listening?

Recently, I had what I thought was an astonishing conversation with an otherwise smart and savvy lady of my acquaintance. She is in her late 30s and professes an interest in marriage and family. She was telling me about a new man in her life, or, rather, a recycled man—someone from her romantic past with whom she had just become reinvolved. "Does he have good character?" I asked, sensing from her cautious description of him that he might be a bit lax in this department.

She repeated the question haltingly, scrunched up her nose, and added a little "Hmm . . ." to the end as she contemplated the answer. "I think he has good character," she replied, "but he has not been living his life that way, do you know what I mean?"

Quite honestly, I didn't. I had always assumed that how you lived your life was a pretty good measure of your character, but since she said it with such a straight face, and the lights were going down in the movie theater, I did not have the opportunity to respond. But even after such a brief interchange, it was clear to me that by rationalizing away her lover's character flaws, this terrific woman was setting herself up for certain heartache down the road.

How accurately we assess people early in our relationships determines the extent to which we will have our needs met later on. Pretend, for example, that you are in the business of selling residential real estate. An enthusiastic yuppie couple bounds into the sales office, eager to know what is available. If you are proficient at your job, you are able to size up the situation effectively, and in a matter of a few minutes you can sense which partner holds the purse strings and which partner wields the emotional power, how viable the couple is financially, how motivated they are to find a new home this very day, and why they may resist a purchase altogether. Your ability to know your customer prevents you from wasting valuable time on professional browsers and helps you outperform the less perceptive salespeople in your office.

I am forced to make similar judgments about people in my work as a relationship coach, since the number of callers who inquire about my program exceeds the number I can effectively accommodate in my schedule. Though I have had hundreds of conversations with prospective clients, I continue to be amazed by the extent to which one brief introductory phone conversation reveals a caller's essential nature—if you are tuned in, that is.

From the caller's tone of voice, choice of vocabulary, line of questioning, sense of humor or lack thereof—even from her answering machine message (should I have occasion to hear it)—I am able to gather a wealth of clues that help me assess whether my services can benefit this particular person. From these nuances I can answer such questions as: Is she open to change? Does she take responsibility for her own happiness? Is she serious about finding a new path? Or is she just a dilettante on the lovelorn circuit? All of this can be grasped in 5 to 15 minutes, and the first impressions that are formed are almost always borne out over time. These same skills can and should be employed in our early interactions with potential mates.

How We Tune In . . . and Out

Let's assume that you are going to a special black-tie event honoring your company's CEO. You may even find yourself seated next to him. Or perhaps you are planning to attend your twentieth college reunion. These special occasions call for a wardrobe adjustment; the dinner dress must be just right. You have a vision in your head, a mental picture you carry from chic boutique to Loehmann's Backroom, and every garment you wriggle into is measured against the Platonic ideal.

You have no thoughts of compromise: If the outfit is not a style that becomes you, if its length does not flatter the leg, if it doesn't fit the function or simply doesn't fit, if the color reminds you too much of your aunt Lil—in short, if it isn't right for you—you walk on by.

How is it, then, that we bring so much clarity to the selection of a cocktail dress and so little wisdom to the crucial business of evaluating men? In part, the explanation is the one contained in the previous chapter: Clarity about others is possible only after we have gained clarity about ourselves. More specifically, however, we have trouble assessing men because we are cut off from the feminine side of our nature.

Looking at the origins of life from the biblical perspective, God made woman from Adam's thirteenth rib. While man came from dead unfeeling earth, so the story goes, woman was fashioned from living matter, endowed with a more feeling and intuitive makeup. Because woman was built from an internal part of a person, she is predisposed to comprehend the entirety of situations from the "inside," suggests psychologist Lisa Aiken. That is, Aiken continues, a woman by nature can see a forest without first having to see all the trees.

Whether or not one subscribes to such theological interpretations, one thing is clear: This primitive feminine ability to perceive reality from the inside is a dormant power that few late-twentieth-century women know how to summon. The contemporary alienation from our essential female natures is what psychologist Toni Grant calls "the crisis in the Madonna," a shutting off of the softer, intuitive, receptive parts of ourselves in favor of the dynamic, striving, mastering parts that we have needed to compete in a male-dominated society. Yet the valves we have shut off to make us stronger in the workplace have left us weakened on the home front: With the receptive side of our nature blocked, we are ill-equipped to absorb the truth about men. We have forgotten how to listen.

I became aware of my own listening deficit when I was dating often and yet feeling no connection to the men in my life. Accustomed to being a managerial woman by day, I had allowed my assertive, in-control style to eat up the night.

A date with me was less a romantic interlude than an exhausting, though lively, summit at which I set out to display the full range of my wit, talents, and accomplishments.

Deep down, I sensed that something about my behavior was working against me. Using a new blind date as an experimental test case, I vowed to leave the driving to him, sit back and enjoy the view, zip my mouth, and see what developed. At first it felt enormously awkward to relinquish control of the proceedings. What if, without me in the lead, things fell apart? I forced myself to smile and encourage as he chatted away, resisting the impulse to rush in and fill the dead spaces in the conversation with the sound of my own voice, allowing him to reveal himself, concentrating on what he was saying between the lines. When I did speak, it was not to impress him but to ask questions that would help me to know him better.

As a receptive vessel rather than a strategic player, I was in a better position to evaluate this man's character; less prone to fantasize, more able to hear the truth, whatever it might be. To be certain, it was useful to practice on someone for whom I had only casual feelings. By the time the stakes had gotten higher, I had turned into a consummate listener. (Of course, this is not to suggest that the man's listening to you isn't important as well. But that's a *different* book.)

It is a special talent to be able to reach accurate conclusions based on the facts. There are many things we want in life, and it is easy to distort the decision-making process in the pursuit of those desires. Therefore, the tendency of women not to hear men clearly is further aggravated by a simple but often overlooked habit of human nature: We are prone to edit out of consciousness what we don't want to hear.

A simple demonstration proves the point. If you flip through *Travel and Leisure* or *Bon Appetit*, what captures your

attention? The places and foods you are already predisposed to like. If pumpkin soup and Arctic cruises are not to
your taste, your eye effortlessly glides over them without
really registering. You automatically delete them from the
page. Conversely, if you bring to the table, so to speak, a passion for pecan pie, you'll not only notice the recipe but convince yourself that the caloric content is less onerous than it
seems. It is not a crime to deceive oneself about a wedge of
pie. But when the self-deception no longer involves a few
extra pounds at the hip line but, rather, a gut-wrenching
mistake made in the name of love, it is time to take stock.

In my single days, I was quite masterful at editing out
data proffered by men that did not jibe with my romantic
dreams. And invariably, the vital facts that had been available to me early in the game but that I had willingly ignored
were the very elements that doomed us as a couple in the
end. I am thinking now of one of my most significant relationships—a volatile, passionate romance with a highly
intelligent, witty, and extremely charming man who was
some years my senior, had never been married, and was
known about town as a ladies' man. Those last few details
alone should have been enough to send a focused woman
packing, but I was, as I say, less enlightened back then.

Our first encounter, a chance meeting at a neighborhood café, was a spirited and flirtatious event between two
people whose natural affinity was hard to mask. The elec-
tricity was palpable. And yet there was a theme to his side of
the conversation that should have been a red flag to me,
and that theme was "options." He referred to them a lot, the
implication being that personal freedom was his mantra
while commitments and obligations—professional and personal—were somewhat akin to death.

The intense, sixteen-month love affair that followed,

and that brought me both pleasure and pain, could have been quashed at the café that very first morning had I been less willing to tune out the warning signs in the service of my romantic hunger. While this man was incredibly smart, stimulating company, and a wonderful lover, he was also a 48-year-old bachelor with a self-professed phobia about the "M" word and no committed desire to overcome it. He was unmarriageable, and in effect he told me so on the day we met. If only I had been listening.

The Curse of Wishful Thinking

"We wander in illusions," says a character from Shakespeare's *Comedy of Errors,* and in the sphere of romance, those illusions are not easily dispelled. Even when we reclaim our receptive female listening skills, even when we vow to factor in all available data, however discordant, we still have a problem assimilating the truth when it comes to men. A common culprit is desperation, or the "I Have to Get Married by 7:30" syndrome. We want what we want now, and if it doesn't quite fit the bill, we will squeeze it to fit, even if it kills us, which it often does.

Anita, a lovely client who struggled with this malady, called me, agitated and perplexed. She had just met a new prospect at a weekend retreat sponsored by the national company for which she worked. She and this man, a 35-year-old who lived in the suburbs with his mother, had spent 20 hours of togetherness in the bucolic countryside outside our city, along with scores of other employees. They had talked, shared, found they had everything in common. This man was perfect for her, Anita felt. She need look no further.

The problem, however, was that since their return from the retreat ten days earlier, he had come into the city from the suburbs twice to see male friends but had not made time to see her. He had taken down her phone number, and even if he had misplaced it, he could have located her easily, because they worked for the same company. Should she confront him? she wondered. This was a promising relationship. How could he be ignoring her?

What was painful for Anita to hear, and what she did not want to hear even though she had consulted me, was that she and this man had no relationship. They had shared a moment in time, yes, but back in the real world he had chosen not to extend it. Perhaps he intended to call her at a later date. But more than likely, he had no such plan.

The original thorny fact remained: He was a 35-year-old man who lived with his mother. This was not a temporary, situational arrangement due to finances or illness, but a permanent lifestyle choice. While this would not be noteworthy in European cultures, where parents and unmarried children sometimes reside together, it should have been an obvious warning signal to an American woman whose agenda was marriage. Of all the single men at the retreat, this deserving lady had targeted an unavailable one. Now that she had invested 20 hours in him—what felt like a lifetime—she wanted it to pay off. She was focused on what could have been. But her bet had been placed on the wrong horse. I advised her to refrain from calling him and to move on.

While men are quite capable of deceiving women in studied and measured ways, they are just as likely to come clean about their limited capacity for commitment and to let women do themselves in. A woman with low self-regard may hear the truth and lie to herself, convinced she won't find another man if she throws this prize catch back to sea.

Several years ago, I had a coworker named Wendy, an

American woman with an open heart, who was madly in love with an Indian foreign service officer who was posted in her city. While he was happy to have Wendy play hostess for his nonstop round of social obligations and to fulfill all the functions of a wife (including sex, of course), he had made it clear to her from the beginning that their cultural differences would preclude his ever marrying her. He intended eventually to return to his country of origin and assume a key role in its government, a career goal that would be denied him if he brought home a foreign wife.

Despite being told the reality up front, Wendy stayed in the relationship, hoping, I suppose, that her sheer devotion would outlast his resistance. Eight years and 500 cocktail parties later, he went back to his native land as originally advertised, and she was left alone, having wasted some of her most precious single years and with nothing to show for it.

This female propensity toward hope against all odds is as old as the creation of woman. For the Greeks, the first woman was a shy maiden whom the gods called Pandora, a name meaning "the gift of all." The common mythology is that the gods gave Pandora a box into which each had put something, though they forbade her from ever looking inside. But as quintessential woman, Pandora was graced with natural curiosity. She had to know what was inside that box!

Finally, she opened the lid and out flew all the dreams and sorrows of mankind. Terrified, Pandora clamped down the lid, but it was too late. Everything had escaped. Everything, that is, except Hope. The Greeks translate this quality as "wishful thinking," and it is this state of wishful thinking that the ancient Greeks believed resides in womankind for eternity.

Psychologists Connell Cowan and Melvyn Kinder, in their best-selling book *Smart Women, Foolish Choices*, speak to the ease with which women infuse wishful thought into their dating lives. In addition to what is said and not said on a first date, say the authors, there are powerful expectations just under the surface—hopes about the kind of man we want to find and fantasies about fulfilling our desire for romance and love. Cowan and Kinder see these deeper desires as little "shadowy companions that can accompany a woman on a date" with a new man.

I can recall a vivid example of my own brand of wishful thinking early in my quest for a mate. A married male colleague, Ted, who took an avid interest in my personal welfare, wanted me to meet a highly eligible man with whom he was doing some business. He described the candidate in question, Jason, as being in his early 40s, educated, kind, handsome, and gifted in his profession. To add fuel to the fire, Jason had also been a star athlete at his alma mater, even weighing briefly an opportunity to turn pro.

We arranged to have a weekday lunch at a restaurant in the building where I worked, and the fine male specimen who walked into my office that day, locking eyes with me as I was wrapping up a telephone call, literally caused me to lose my train of thought. After this, who needed to eat?

Yet within the first 30 minutes of our lunch, it was apparent from Jason's conversation and his mannerisms that this seductive man was also troubled, a conflicted person who, despite his many achievements, had not repaired the damage of an unhealthy childhood or sustained a lasting intimate relationship in adulthood. As we munched on salad Niçoise and flirted shamelessly, I remember saying to myself these very words: "I hope he is not as neurotic as he seems." A wishful thought if ever there was one!

Of course, Jason turned out to be even more so. While I did not waste a lot of time coming to this sad conclusion, I need never have ventured into such a no-win arena at all. I had accurately perceived the truth at the debut lunch but had allowed wishful thinking to override my own good sense.

Toxic Romance

For some women, it is purely a desire to be swept away by romance that causes them to ignore obvious early warning signs about a man's character in favor of transitory qualities that titillate and delight. The following story illustrates just how wantonly a woman can place herself on a romantic ledge, despite having all the disturbing facts at her disposal.

A few years ago, my friend Sandra fell under the spell of a married man whom I knew professionally. I could understand the attraction, for Tim was a sexy, dynamic executive, a man on the way up who knew how to please a woman—so much so that I was privy to details of some of his prior conquests and a few broken hearts that had been left in their wake.

Aside from the fact that Tim was currently married and unavailable, he was a man who would always be unavailable. He was a person who wove complications into all his romantic alliances so that he would never have to be truly intimate with anyone. This was a man who could function only as part of a triangle.

Sandra knew this about him, not only because I had told her, but also because she was an accomplished listener when it came to men, and she had picked up some useful clues during their first encounter. When she came to me for advice, knowing in her heart that pursuit of him was folly, I counseled her to steer clear and under no circumstances to fall in love. It would come to no good, not only because he was married—reason enough to keep one's hands off!—but also because he would never be a one-woman man.

But my logic was a poor match for the elaborate romantic fantasies that were already in high gear. Claiming to recognize the risks and yet be willing to live with the consequences, Sandra plunged headlong into a love affair, charmed him into leaving his wife, and in short order was installed as wife number two. The postscript could have written itself: Several years later, while she was waiting to give birth to their first child, she discovered Tim was involved with another woman he had met while on an assignment abroad.

"Why didn't I listen?" she lamented the night she gave us girls the gruesome details. She remembered not only everything about the conversation she and I had shared, but also the clear warning signals she had picked up from Tim when they first met. Fortunately for Sandra, she came away from the experience with a beautiful baby girl, but there were surely less painful ways to become a mother. (The story does have a happy ending, however. After divorcing Tim, she eventually married a man who valued her and who became a devoted stepfather to her child.)

Sandra's instincts had been good, but she had ignored them. This is an all too common roadblock to good decision-making for many women. In a culture in which women have been taught to preserve harmony at the expense of expressing their authentic feelings, some of us don't respect our gut when it tells us something is awry in the early stages of a relationship.

A new client came to me with the express purpose of wanting to break up with her boyfriend, a man with whom she had been involved for some years. From the beginning of their relationship, the man had been separated but not divorced. At age 36, Pamela had finally admitted to herself that he would never close the books on his previous marriage and marry her.

What was especially upsetting to Pamela was that she had suspected this about him from day one, but she had not respected her own instincts and had instead moved easily into a dead-end romance. Pretty and bright, Pamela nevertheless second-guessed herself in many areas of her life. Once she got over her anger at herself for wasting so much time, she was able to sever the ties with her companion and focus on men whose slates were clean.

Theologian Dov Heller distills the subject of listening to its essence: To make good choices, he offers, we must operate from a position of truth. If we don't listen, if we lie to ourselves, functioning from a position of fantasy or wish rather than truth, we are guaranteed to make bad choices. It takes discipline and work to look at what is real, rather than to focus on what is merely comfortable or comforting. But the effort pays off in the quality of life we lead and the health of the relationships we forge.

The 15-Minute Test

To demonstrate for yourself how easily you may have fallen into one of the nonlistening patterns described above, create a sample grid, using a piece of lined paper. In the first column, enter the names of former spouses and significant former lovers. In the center column, next to each name, enter your best recollection of your first 15 minutes with that person. What information did he give you about himself? What were your impressions and reactions, both to what was said and to what was omitted? What were your overall feelings about this man? What about him did you like best? Least? In the last column, explain the factors that ultimately led to the relationship's demise. Women who do this exercise are usually astonished to find how frequently the seeds of destruction were evident in the very first encounter.

The 15-minute test can also be applied in reverse. That is, it can illuminate the early signs of potential in a healthy relationship. For example, to be highly promising, an initial encounter with a man should inspire some degree of relaxation. What such a mood suggests is: This person has no agenda, he is what he seems, I can be myself with him. Can this assumption occasionally mislead us? Of course. No system is 100 percent foolproof. But if you begin with the premise that a man's company should put you at ease, not agitate you or set you immediately on fire, you will be starting from a position of power. Your ears will not betray you. It is from this vantage point that good decisions can be made and that good outcomes can flow.

Ask contentedly married women to recall their first meetings with their spouses—what impressions and observations stick out with regard to the initial exposure? While few say it was love at first sight (since instant love is rarely real), they invariably remember something wholesome or down-to-earth about their man: his genuineness, his honesty or lack of pretense, the degree to which he made them laugh or feel at ease.

Danielle, who just celebrated her tenth anniversary, cites her husband's kindness, confidence, and humanistic spirit as qualities that first struck her about him. He was very open, she continues, with no artifice. Danielle realized almost immediately that they shared compatible values, that they viewed the world with a similar lens.

Trish, also solidly married, remembers her blind date with her husband as being equally revealing. She met him at a time when he was at several personal crossroads. His mother had recently died, his father was ill, and after some professional losses, his business needed to be realigned. It was clear he was a nice man, says his wife in retrospect. She could tell this was someone who was open about his feelings, someone who wanted to share his feelings with another person. And, she continues, this man's insecure parts—which he did not try to hide—were the endearing grace notes that captured her heart.

My first meeting with my now-husband proved instructive as well, for within the space of 15 minutes he gave me a lot of insight into his character. I knew from his presentation and naturalness that he was wholesome, straightforward, and accessible. He seemed the type of person who was incapable of the jaded gamesmanship that clouds so much of the modern dating horizon, and indeed time proved this impression to be correct. Boring? Some women hooked on fantasy and danger might say so, but I knew I had finally met a real man, not an ersatz one. I felt as though I had finally come home.

A Time to Talk and a Time to Listen

Earlier in this chapter, I described an exercise I used on a blind date when I consciously refrained from talking too much and instead focused on really listening. Eventually, this style of behavior with a new man became second nature to me. That is why I was able to absorb a lot of revealing information proffered by my now-husband during our first 15 minutes together. Had I been in a nonlistening mode, I might have missed these essential clues about his nature, and I might have passed up a good man as a result.

If you applied the 15-minute test to important relationships from your past and the test results indicate that you are not a careful listener, it is time to learn a new skill. If you often do recognize the early warning signals in the first 15 minutes with a new man, but frequently disregard them, it is time to get tougher with yourself. Here are two exercises that can help.

1: Force yourself to be quiet on your next first date or first encounter with a new man, listening both to what is being said and to what is being left out. Afterward, write down all your initial impressions of this man, together with the concrete information that he shared. Is there anything about what you know so far that is troubling or should be viewed as a red flag? How do you plan to check out these gray areas further? What would you need to know to make you believe in this man's worthiness as a marital prospect?

2: In the previous chapter, I suggested you compile your personal master list of deal-breakers and deal-optionals as they apply to potential marital candidates. Review that list now. Memorize it. After every date or encounter with a new eligible man, make a new list of the signals given and statements made by this particular man, as well as your general impressions of him. Compare this list with your master list of deal-breakers and deal-optionals. If your fundamental needs from a mate are at odds with who this man seems to be, he is not an appropriate marital prospect for you.

Part 2

Good Things Happen When You Get Out of Your Own Way

5

Our Own Little Pharaohs Keep Us in Bondage: Creating Your Personal Profile

The Old Testament Book of Exodus tells us that not all the Jews who were enslaved to Pharaoh in Egypt wanted to escape their bondage. While slavery was unpleasant, it was familiar. Choosing to leave for the Promised Land meant wandering in a desert, confronting the unknown. For some, this was too frightening a prospect. So they stayed behind, a choice for safety, but safety without the possibility of joy and fulfillment.

It is hard to have new social experiences or to develop a new mind-set if one is enslaved to old habits and behaviors that restrict opportunity, sap one's spirit, and control one's life. Personal tyrants can be internal as well as external and take many forms: an addiction to people or substances that are unhealthy; an overreliance on work, status, material possessions, or physical beauty for self-regard; or even something as seemingly benign as dependence on family or familiar friends to fill up one's calendar. When we get in touch with the ways we enslave ourselves—and work to become more liberated from them—we "clear the decks," so to speak. When personal tyrants no longer rule us, we become receptive to a broader range of feelings and experiences. This means we also become more open to potential mates.

To track down where such impediments may be lurking in your own life (and we all have them!), fill out the following Personal Profile, using separate sheets of lined paper on which you have listed the numbers from 1 to 75. The questions are designed to help you think about how you have been living, what priorities and values you have been emphasizing, and how some of these choices may conflict with your marital goals.

When I work with private clients face-to-face and pose these same questions, I have the advantage of being able to ask follow-up questions when the client's response is tentative or murky. This added step gives the client a more complete picture of what is actually going on in her life. Since I cannot be with you while you complete the profile, try to approach the exercise as though I were there. In other words, don't let yourself off the hook! Like a good workout at the gym, the process should force you to stretch. If your first response to a question is "I don't know" or "I'm not sure," rephrase the question and push yourself to find a possible answer. "I don't know" is not an answer. It is usually an evasion.

Respond as honestly and as thoroughly as you can. This is not a test. It is an exercise that can help you derive more pleasure and satisfaction from life. Later in the chapter we will assess some of your responses.

Personal Profile

1. Age? _____ **2.** Occupation?_____

3. How many hours do you work per week?_____

4. Education?_____

5. Years in current city? _____

6. Previously married? _____ How long? _____
How long ago?_____

7. Divorced?_____Widowed?_____ Children?_____
Ages?_____ Want children? _____

8. Previous live-in relationships other than
marriage?_____ How long?_____

9. Previous long-term, serious relationships other than
live-in?_____
How long?_____

10. How would you describe your parents' marriage?
(Be as specific as possible.)_____

_____

_____

11. Do you have siblings? _____

Where do you fit in the family constellation? _____

12. Good health? _____ Drink? _____ Smoke? _____

13. Hobbies and interests?

_____

_____

14. How many hours per week do you spend on your hobbies and interests? _____

15. How often do you socialize?

Often? _____ Occasionally?_____ Rarely? _____

16. How often do you pursue self-oriented activities (classes, hobbies, etc.)? _____

17. How important is physical fitness to your life?

Very? _____ Somewhat? _____ Not very? _____

18. What kinds of things do you do to stay fit?

_____

_____

19. Are you affiliated with a church or synagogue? _____

20. If previously married, is your ex still in your life? _____

How so? _____

21. Do you have close family living nearby? _____

Parents? _____ Siblings? _____ Children? _____

Other? _____

22. How much time per week do you spend with them?

_____

23. How much time per week do you spend with good

friends?_____

24. Do you surround yourself with supportive friends and

family?_____

25. Do you have pets? _____ How important are they to

your life? _____

26. If you have cat(s), where do you keep the box of kitty

litter? _____

What do you do to keep your home free of cat smells,

hairs, etc.? _____

Does the cat sleep with you? _____

27. If you have dog(s), does the dog sleep with you?

_____

If the dog sleeps with you, what happens with the dog

if/when you have an overnight guest?

_____

28. Do you like to spend time alone? _____

Often? _____ Occasionally? _____ Rarely? _____

29. If you prefer to be alone, why?

_____

If you dislike being alone, why?

_____

30. Are you involved in any volunteer or charity work?

_____

31. How much time per week do you devote to it?

_____

32. If a friend dropped in on you unexpectedly, would your refrigerator contain items from which to make an impromptu dinner? _____

33. When you sleep in your bed, do you take up the entire width or stick to "your side"? _____

34. How many comfortable places to sit are there in the primary public rooms of your living space? _____

Describe

_____

_____

35. Describe the chairs and their degree of comfort in your primary eating room (kitchen or dining room).

_____

_____

36. Do you have photos on display featuring ex-spouses and boyfriends? _____ Do you have photos on display featuring family and friends other than former spouses or boyfriends? _____

37. When was the last time you purchased fresh flowers for your home? _____

38. How *neat* is your home environment?

Very? _____ Quite? _____ Only a little? _____

Not at all? _____

39. How *clean* is your home environment?

Very? _____ Quite? _____ Only a little? _____

Not at all? _____

40. In your bedroom, is there a reading light on both sides of the bed, or on yours alone? _____

41. Is there a night table or other surface on both sides of the bed, or on yours alone? _____

42. If you are petite, is your furniture also small-scale?

_____

If you are tall, is your furniture oversized? _____

43. Describe your ideal living environment.

_____

_____

44. To what extent does your home environment conform to this description?

_____

_____

45. How important are your physical surroundings to your personal happiness?

Very? _____ Quite? _____ A little? _____

Not at all? _____

46. Does your living space have bookshelves? _____

Is the lighting in your home on single switches or can you adjust the levels for "mood" lighting? _____

Are your towels soft enough to wrap a baby in? _____

47. What comments, if any, have members of the opposite sex made about your living space (positive or negative)?

_____

_____

48. How would you describe your home environment?

Casual? _____ Formal? _____ Modern? _____

Traditional? _____ Tailored? _____ Romantic? _____

49. Are you currently in a serious relationship? _____

If yes, how long has it been going on? _____

50. Do you want to marry him? _____

Why do you think you haven't?

_____

If you do not want to marry him, why are you continu-

ing the relationship?

_____

51. Are you currently dating? _____ Do you date one to

two times per week? _____ One to two times per

month? _____ One to two times per year? _____

52. When you meet someone you like and start to date,

what is the usual time frame for the relationship to

become sexually intimate?

First date? _____ Second date? _____

After one to two months? _____

After three months? _____ Other? _____

53. Are you sexually active? _____

Do you want to be? _____

54. If you are not currently dating, how long has it been since you dated? _____

55. Have you been involved with married men? _____
Never? _____ Rarely? _____
Occasionally? _____ Frequently? _____

56. Fill in the blank: I always seem to get involved with men who

_____

_____

(If you honestly do not see a pattern to your relationships, write "not applicable.")

57. What methods have you pursued to find a mate?
Fix-ups? _____ Dating services? _____
Personals? _____ Matchmakers? _____
Other? _____

58. How much time per week do you spend thinking about your personal life? _____

59. How much time per week do you spend doing something about it? _____

60. What kinds of things do you do?

_____

61. What do you want in a mate?

_____

_____

62. What do you need in a mate?

_____

_____

63. On a scale of 1 to 10, with 10 being most important,
rate the following qualities in terms of their relative
importance to you with regard to a potential mate:

Education?_____ Honesty? _____ Fidelity? _____

Integrity? _____ Physically fit? _____Age? _____

Shared interests? _____ Shared values? _____

Shared religion? _____ Spirituality? _____

Locale? _____ Income? _____

Independence? _____ No prior kids? _____

Open to kids? _____ Sense of humor? _____

Communicative? _____ Flexibility? _____

Tolerance? _____ Patience? _____ Kindness? _____

Generosity? _____ Intelligence? _____

64. What five adjectives would you use to describe yourself?

_____

_____

65. What is your best trait? _____

Your worst trait? _____

66. On a scale of 1 to 10, with 10 being the first trait listed in each pair, how optimistic or pessimistic are you? _____ How assertive or passive? _____ How much a leader or follower? _____ How easygoing or rigid and controlling? _____

67. List three things about yourself that would make you a good marital partner.

_____

_____

68. List three things about yourself that would make you a challenging marital partner.

_____

_____

69. Of the three things that would make you a challenging marital partner, which ones would you be willing to work on or modify in the interest of forging a fulfilling marriage?

_____

_____

Why haven't you already done so?

_____

70. How have you changed in the last five years?

_____

_____

71. Why do you want to get married?

_____

_____

72. Why do you feel you haven't found a mate?

_____

_____

73. Which statement more accurately reflects your true feelings? "I'm afraid I will never find someone to marry," or "I know it's hard to find someone to marry, but I believe he is out there."

_____

74. To what extent do you feel you may stand in your own way?

_____

How so?

_____

75. My life would be more satisfying if

_____

Evaluating Your Answers

Your completed Personal Profile can be viewed as a sort of X-ray of the structure of your life. The overall picture reveals not only where you have chosen to center your energies but also what areas of life you have chosen to ignore, either consciously or by default. Ideally, the X-ray would illuminate a balanced life, but it is an ideal precisely because so few of us live in true harmony with our needs. In addition, the profile highlights trouble spots, bad habits, and destructive patterns you may now wish to examine up close as a prelude to becoming a more marriage-focused—and marriage-able—woman. Let us explore some of your responses.

Question 3 addresses the amount of time you currently devote to your work—a topic that Chapter Seven explores in greater depth. If you work in excess of 40 hours per week, you need to assess honestly why you allow work to dominate your life. Does your livelihood depend on your working long and taxing hours? Would your work product or your salary suffer in *dramatic* ways if you were to cut back somewhat? Does the extra salary afforded you by these long hours make up for your loss of freedom, relaxation, and time for a satisfying personal life? Or—be candid—do you work long hours to avoid having a personal life?

Since knights on horseback do not come knocking at one's door, women who wish to marry in midlife need the time and energy to proactively meet eligible men. A harried, stressed-out woman cannot put her best foot forward to try on a glass slipper, let alone to enjoy an after-work date! If the demands of your work deplete you of time and energy, and if you sincerely wish to marry, it is mandatory that you reorder your priorities. Virtually none of the women I've known who married in midlife were workaholics at the time they met their husbands; however, in many cases, the women were reformed workaholics whose good fortunes on the marital front were direct consequences of their having made room for personal fulfillment in their lives.

Question 7 asks whether you still wish to have children. If your answer is a definite yes, then any man for whom this desire is a problem is the wrong man for you. As noted in an earlier chapter, once one's spousal deal-breakers are firmly fixed in mind, all decisions must be measured against those articulated needs. A man who says he does not want children, or who already has children and does not want more, or who simply dislikes children altogether, is an obvious mismatch.

Women frequently deceive themselves into believing that a resistant man will change his mind on this issue in the name of love. But, more often, the woman ends up compromising her dreams in the interest of preserving the relationship. And rare is the woman who makes this adaptation without later resenting the man for denying her the experience of motherhood. In truth, it is she who made the unfortunate bargain. If you are unclear where a new man in your life stands on the issue of children, ask. And if his answer does not square with your deepest needs, move on.

Your view of your parents' relationship (question 10) can be a window into your own expectations, assumptions, and fears about marriage. Of the women I have worked with, a solid 25 percent describe their parents' unions as having been "strong," "enduring," "loving." But a larger percentage of women paint a less flattering portrait of their marriage models, which they perceived as "lacking in intimacy," "okay, but joyless," or just plain "lousy." These women refer to passive fathers who were dominated by striving mothers; mothers whose investment in their children eclipsed their involvement with their mates; fathers so wrapped up in their work that their wives became invisible; relationships characterized by bickering or disinterest; and occasionally, no harmony at all, as summed up by one client when she said, "They fought for 55 years."

It is useful to make an objective appraisal of how the marriage model in your home may have influenced your current marital status. Have you idealized a solid, healthy marriage—so much so that you do not want to risk falling short of the mark? Do patterns in your own behavior with men mirror destructive behaviors you witnessed at home? Somewhere along the line, did you decide that marriage was too painful or too much work, thereby dodging intimacy altogether? Everyone's answer will be different, and no single answer is the whole story. But acknowledging the imprint left by your parents' marriage contributes to your own understanding of the choices you have made on the home front.

Hobbies and interests (questions 13 and 14) are to be pursued. We often characterize ourselves as having various hobbies and interests when, in fact, we've allotted no quality time for enjoying them. If you listed a variety of activities in question 13, but found in question 14 that you devote little time to them, your time management skills need honing. A commitment to activities beyond your work and family obligations makes you a more interesting—and interested—person. And having creative and recreational outlets increases your opportunities for social contact with eligible men. Do not shortchange yourself in this department.

Question 19 queries your affiliation with a church or synagogue—environments that offer not only spiritual nourishment but also social interaction and exposure to like-minded singles. If you've never set foot in a church or synagogue, I'm not necessarily suggesting you start going now. Nor am I advocating using these institutions solely for the purpose of meeting men. But even if you're a doubter, church or synagogue can provide an enriching sense of community. How one can best use such organizational affiliations will be delineated in Chapter Nine. In brief, houses of worship sponsor a broad range of activities, usually at moderate cost. Allowing a spiritual dimension into one's life can be a refreshing respite from the frantic pace most of us maintain. The calming influence of such moments of reflection adds serenity to one's being, a magnetic quality that men notice and appreciate.

Many women chafe at the notion of looking for a man in a house of worship, shortsightedly believing the idea to be hokey or uncool. Personally, I'd be delighted to have a hundred dollars for every married woman I know who met her husband in just this fashion. For the most part, religious institutions are safe, protected environments in which to meet new marital candidates. And an added bonus is that the minister, priest, or rabbi can be consulted on a confidential basis to introduce you to available men, or to vouch for the character of someone you may have already met. Women who wonder where all the good men have gone would do well to look in these very corridors; a man who is able to make a commitment to a belief system beyond himself is likely to be able to make a commitment to a woman as well.

Questions 20 through 24 inquire into your network of close family and friends. A woman wishing to marry in midlife needs family and friends who support and nurture her goals, not who work against them. Some clients who find it difficult to meet appropriate men also turn out to be locked into unsatisfying relationships with people in general, or with disgruntled single women whose chief pastime is harping and complaining about men.

Getting off this unpleasant treadmill requires radical surgery to one's social sphere. If you aren't socializing with people who bolster your goals, it is time to get new friends. There is no surer way to stay single than to surround yourself with malcontents, victims, or nay-sayers. They merely drag you down.

A second trap involves the opposite condition: family or friends who are so nurturing that one has little incentive to venture outside their cozy embrace. If you have close family living nearby and have made them the center of your universe, you may be relying on them at the expense of developing an autonomous life. It is difficult for new experiences—and, by extension, new men—to come your way if your free time is consumed by comfortable but limiting family activities—a theme that Chapter Eight explores in depth.

Pets are a matter of passion for those who have and love them. But "Love me, love my cat" may be too big a leap for an otherwise worthy marriage candidate. Questions 25 through 27 speak to this issue. If your pet functions as a clear member of the animal kingdom while providing you good company, then you are fortunate indeed. However, if your pet has become a virtual substitute for intimacy with human beings, beware. You may soon sprout whiskers!

A box of redolent kitty litter may be unobjectionable to the proud owner of a prize-winning Persian, but for the rest of us it is an odor worth avoiding. Your home should smell fresh and enticing, not like a pet shop. Therefore, kitty litter belongs in an out-of-the-way spot—on a service porch, for example—not in your kitchen or guest bath. Cat hairs need not grace your furniture, or your bedsheets. The goal, after all, is to be available for *human* relations.

I once dated a man who had a gigantic Old English sheep dog named Elvira. Elvira was extremely loving and friendly, so much so that she would jump to greet a stranger, knocking down all but the most sturdy visitor. But her enthusiasms did not stop there. Undisciplined and overindulged by her owner, poor Elvira would continue to jump, maul, and dominate—antics that ceased only when, at the eleventh hour and after the repeated urging of the guest, her master eventually removed the animal to an outdoor dog run.

What became clear after I knew this man a little better was that Elvira was a wife substitute. Her presence was overpowering, and her owner liked it that way. The dog was a convenient impediment to intimacy. If your pet serves a similar purpose in your life, you may be less ready for marriage than you claim.

Questions 28 and 29 relate to your attraction to or aversion to spending time alone. To get married one first has to date (sorry!), and to date one has to be willing to leave the house (apologies again!). These harsh realities can be a drag for the entrenched midlife single who would prefer to spend an evening at home in a bathrobe, eating takeout Chinese and watching *I Love Lucy* reruns.

I had a delightful 36-year-old client, Kim, who truly wished to be married and yet rarely left her apartment. Further, she worked as a freelance artist, which meant she could earn a living without ever setting foot outside. Shy and reticent but blessed with a delicious sense of humor and feminine charm, this woman admitted that she spent so much time alone because it was "easier"; she had spun a cocoon to ward off the anxiety of unsettling social interactions. To lift her from this untenable rut, I prodded her to move her office outside her home—into a building occupied by other independent contractors such as herself.

Once she made the move, her social life improved, for she was finally visible to other people!

To be certain, enjoying some solitary time has a positive value, because it builds independence and self-reliance. But beyond that, the midlife single who wants to wed must remain in circulation. There is no other way.

Questions 30 and 31 address your involvement in volunteer or charity work. A commitment to such endeavors pays off in a multitude of ways: It forces you to focus away from yourself and your own problems; it makes a valuable contribution to the welfare of others and to the community at large; and it has the added bonus of bringing you into contact with other civic-minded individuals—some of whom are bound to be single men.

Deciding to become active in a charitable cause does not mean you must be relegated to licking envelopes, though this is valuable volunteerism as well. If you seek a more stimulating form of involvement, analyze how your own professional or personal skills might be useful in the nonprofit world, and offer your free services accordingly. Most charitable organizations are desperate for volunteers in areas as diverse as fund-raising, public relations, event planning, newsletter writing, advertising, and hands-on involvement with clientele. You do not have to be an expert, you need only be competent and committed.

Questions 32 through 48 investigate your feelings about your home and your home environment. Architecture professor Clare Cooper Marcus has been studying this subject for some 20 years, believing that the choices we make about our home and its contents are like little messages from the unconscious—reflections of what we really feel. In fact, Marcus contends that our home environments can actually foster or stifle our psychic growth.

By way of example, return to question 36 ("Do you have photos on display featuring ex-spouses and boyfriends?"). If you answered yes, you might well ask yourself, "What for?" While it can be assumed that a mature single woman has a past, she need not memorialize her romantic history for new suitors. If you have children with a former spouse and his smiling face happens to pop up in between theirs in a framed photo on your coffee table, no harm done. But, in general, erecting a photographic homage to your romantic past will be a turnoff to new men. And if you truly wish to move forward in your personal life, keeping leftover lovers on display merely delays your progress by letting you live in the past—or worse, by encouraging you to idealize it. Besides, if these old lovers were such terrific guys, how come they're no longer around?

I have a dear friend, Leslie, who was a single divorcée for a number of years before finally marrying again in her mid-40s. Leslie, a free spirit who had led an extraordinarily colorful and adventurous life, had a refrigerator plastered with snapshots of various male friends and former lovers— most of them handsome, tanned, strapping Adonises maneuvering catamarans or paddling canoes; beautiful male specimens cavorting on the beach in Malibu or schussing their way down the slopes in Vermont. Even *I* found these pictures a bit intimidating, and I wasn't dating her! So I often wondered how a new man in her life might feel when confronted by these images as he freshened his drink or watched Leslie cook. Surely this visual assault could not have been confidence-inspiring for most of the men who crossed my friend's threshold.

Questions 41 and 42 measure how territorial you are and how willing—or unwilling—you may be to share your living space. If you have a reading light and end table or surface on "your side" of the bed, but have not bothered to make the other side comfortable for a potential partner, then you may be less interested in having company than you think. This is a minor observation, to be sure, but these small indices add up. Take stock of your living environment for its overall message. Is it new-man friendly? Or is the unspoken message more readily a warning that a visitor need not get too comfortable?

The living space of a very petite single woman I know sends out just such a message, for her answer to question 42 ("If you are petite, is your furniture also small-scale?") would be a resounding yes. So tiny is the ultrafeminine, Munchkin-like furniture in her living room that any man of reasonable size might suspect he had just fallen down the rabbit hole in *Alice in Wonderland* and was now a guest at the Mad Hatter's tea party. No doubt, the initial effect can be quite charming—appealing to a man's natural curiosity and to his attraction to the unpredictable. But once the novelty wears off, the average-sized visitor more probably experiences tired muscles and a dire need for a good stretch. This is not an environment conducive to long visits.

Questions 43 and 44 explore how closely your actual living environment conforms to your ideal one. If your fantasy extends to something on the order of the royal palace in Monaco, then there is little hope of reconciling the ideal with the pedestrian. But if your conception of the perfect living space is something less grand, there is hope that you could bring your ideal into harmony with your reality, thus giving yourself some of what you want.

I am surprised by the number of clients whose ideals are within reach, but who nonetheless fail to give themselves any of what they want—often because they do not feel they deserve to be comfortable or content. If your ideal is an apartment with lots of light, or a small house with open spaces rather than tiny connecting rooms, or simply a living room with vases of fresh tulips, take serious stock of what keeps you from realizing your vision. If the impediment is financial, do some legwork and determine whether a scaled-down version of your dream might be within your budget. If the stumbling block is psychological, examine why you resist a positive change that could add so much pleasure to your everyday existence.

Finally, revisit your answer to question 47, which asks what comments members of the opposite sex have made with regard to your living space. First and foremost, your home must please you. But if you would like to marry, potential candidates must also feel comfortable on your turf. A new man should not only enjoy spending time in your living space, he should be able to imagine spending a lot *more* time there; the environment should beckon him rather than hold him at bay. There is no magic formula for making a man feel at home in your midst. And, of course, most of his comfort will depend on your comfort with each other. But, all things being equal, a wise single woman makes her home an inviting, serene place to be—for herself as well as for company.

Question 52, addressing the time frame in which your relationships customarily become physically intimate, deserves special attention. While about half of my clients say they become intimate with a man after one to two months, a fair percentage reveal that their relationships become inti-mate after only three or four dates. Chapter Eleven takes up this topic in greater detail, but suffice it to say that a midlife single woman who is this casual about her sexual involve-ments deserves to stay single. One can make a moral argu-ment in favor of delaying sexual involvement until a relationship is on solid footing. But the practical, commonsense reasons to refrain are equally compelling, as we shall soon see.

If you find yourself becoming involved with the same type of man repeatedly, the pattern should show up in your response to question 56. Most of my clients do perceive a pattern to their romantic choices—and these patterns are usually at odds with their marital goals. Among the most frequently cited are men who can't commit, are emotionally unavailable, are immature, are too needy, or are just not right for the woman—often because she became involved with him too quickly, without first ascertaining his appropriateness, or because she began a relationship with the man because of her own loneliness rather than a genuine interest in him as a person.

Such unproductive patterns of behavior are colossal time-wasters, and as has been already established, the midlife single who is seeking marriage must fiercely conserve her time. If you identify with one of the unproductive patterns listed above—or with an unproductive pattern all your own—call a personal life time-out and get professional help. Do not settle for less than full recovery from these fruitless, repetitive behaviors.

Question 57 asks what methods you have used to meet eligible men—dating services, matchmakers, fix-ups, and so forth. If you are currently pursuing all these avenues, you should be commended for your proactive approach to finding a mate. If you have not tried any of these options—or have tried only some—honestly evaluate what holds you back.

If the roadblock is financial, remember that fees for dating services and matchmakers are *always* negotiable. A published tariff or rate schedule means far less than your personal pitch to the person in charge. These business ventures need clients, and a reduced-rate client is better than none at all. Indicate what you are able to pay, and strike a bargain that works for both of you. Of course, you will be far more successful if you negotiate these terms in person and not by phone.

If your resistance to some of these methods of meeting men is emotional, review Part I of this book while reminding yourself that you have everything to gain and nothing to lose by taking action. If you have already tried these methods of meeting men, but have not done so in a while, commit yourself to a fresh effort. What may not have worked for you two years ago can work for you now, because you come armed with a stronger point of view and a deeper resolve.

Question 63 examines which qualities are most important to you in a potential mate. Review your answer to this question and note which qualities you rated most highly. For the sake of argument, let us assume that your top-rated traits were shared values, generosity, sense of humor, honesty, and education. Now, think about your past relationships with men. Did these men rate highly in the categories you deem most important? Did you assess their attributes before entering into these relationships? Or did you notice what was missing only after diving in? In the future, keep your written list of deal-breakers and deal-optionals that we first discussed in Chapter Three in your wallet or datebook. Referring to the list from time to time reminds you of your true needs in a man and helps you evaluate new prospects.

Question 66 addresses your levels of optimism vs. pessimism, assertiveness vs. passivity, and so forth. My clients frequently respond to this question with a divided answer: They see themselves as assertive, optimistic leaders in their work lives, but far more passive and out-of-control in their personal lives. If you responded along similar lines, pick one category in the personal life sphere that needs strengthening and begin to work on it. You did not become assertive on the job without practice, so give yourself an equal opportunity to evolve into an assertive woman after hours.

For virtually 98 percent of my clients, question 70 ("How have you changed in the last five years?") elicits positive responses. Some of the changes are subtle ones, ranging from "I have let go of my need to control" to "I am more independent and self-confident" to "I am not as driven in my work or as materialistic." For other clients, change means having overcome massive odds, such as one woman who recovered from a near-fatal illness after a harrowing brush with death, and another woman, severely overweight all her life, who shed in excess of 100 pounds and began a normal existence for the first time in 37 years.

If your response to question 70 reveals that you, too, have made strides in becoming a more productive, attractive, and fulfilled person, then give yourself credit for having moved in a positive direction. Furthermore, view the progress you made in your particular arenas of growth as indicative of the kinds of changes you still can make in other facets of your life.

"Why do you want to get married," question 71 asks. If you are truly ready for marriage, your answer centers on your positive needs and desires—and yours alone. While most of my clients respond appropriately, there are some who say they wish to marry to make up for some lack: They feel they *should* marry; they think there is something wrong with them if they do not marry; they believe marriage will make them more acceptable to friends or family; or they wish to be taken care of or to be rescued. Of course, these are all poor reasons to seek a mate. A healthy desire to marry emanates from an affirmative desire to blend one's strengths with those of another.

Your desire for marriage in midlife has a better chance of being actualized if your answer to question 73 (asking whether you believe there is a man out there for you) was optimistic. I am not suggesting that you become a Pollyanna, blind to the realities of the singles marketplace and to the challenges inherent in finding a midlife mate. To pretend that any of this is easy denies the obvious. Indeed, if the assignment were that simple, no one would need a book such as this one! But to be mindful of the challenges while maintaining an upbeat belief in a favorable outcome means you imbue your search with positive energy. There is no wasted motion or squandered gesture. Everything counts. You function at peak capacity.

To use an analogy from your childhood, think about the times you were pushed on a swing. The adult pushing you did not fight the flow of the swing by exerting random force, because this would have gotten you nowhere. Rather, the person pushing made the effort at precisely the moment the swing was already moving forward. By allowing no counterenergy to cancel out your progress—by maximizing the expenditure of effort—the adult helped your swing reach its maximum height. Similarly, your search for a partner reaches its highest potential when its forward thrust is not impeded by negativism and self-doubt.

Your answer to the final question ("My life would be more satisfying if . . . ") most probably includes the finding of a mate. The wise woman knows that a mate will not solve her problems, or magically change her life, or change her into something she is not. What a partner can do, and the reason to conscientiously seek one, is bring a sense of balance and perspective to the table, lend a sympathetic ear and a willing and devoted heart. No man makes a woman's life perfect. If it is perfection you chase, you had best focus on the promise of an afterlife. But fulfillment, yes! It is not only possible but within your grasp. And as you begin to free yourself from whatever personal pharaohs have held you back, you will sense the power in your own hands. To that end, the remaining chapters of this book are designed to help broaden your reach.

6

"He's a Real Nowhere Man"

"Everybody on this ship is in love. Love me whether or not I love you. Love me whether I am fit to love. Love me whether I am able to love. Even if there is no such thing as love. Love me."

—Vivien Leigh in *Ship of Fools*, screenplay by Abby Mann; based on the novel by Katherine Anne Porter

One of the classic ways in which women foil their own marital intentions is by wasting time and emotions on Nowhere Men. Nowhere Men come in a variety of models and disguises.

The Carrie Fisher character in *When Harry Met Sally* has a married lover who will never leave his wife. That's a Nowhere Man. But a man does not have to be married to someone else to be nowhere. The man whom a woman has been dating for four years, who still won't make a marital commitment, is nowhere. The moody CPA who resents his girlfriend's young children, can't be counted on in a crisis, and lets her pick up the check because he pays alimony to two ex-wives, is nowhere. The 40-year-old man who doesn't share the rent and turns down a succession of jobs because they are beneath him, yet expects his partner to be patient while he "finds himself," is, you guessed it, nowhere, too. Trouble is, most Nowhere Men can almost pass for benign, and that is what makes it so lethal to associate with them. In a heartbeat, many women talk themselves into believing that the behavior of these self-centered types is perfectly acceptable. It is not acceptable. Furthermore, continuing to date Nowhere Men gets women nowhere fast.

Strangely, even women blessed with a multitude of choices for male companionship can gravitate toward these bad apples. Henry James's protagonist Isabel Archer, in the classic nineteenth-century novel *The Portrait of a Lady*, is just such a woman. Single and beautiful, this young American heiress surveys her fine choices of suitors—Caspar Goodwood, a solid, upstanding American, and Lord Warburton, a wealthy nobleman desperately in love with her—and instead of selecting one of these exemplary candidates, she picks Gilbert Osmond, an opportunistic fortune hunter.

Gilbert Osmond is an empty shell, but Isabel's imagination fills in all his gaps with substance of her own making. All those who wish Isabel well are opposed to her marrying Osmond, but she naively marries him anyway, only to regret the decision years later when his true nature becomes apparent to her. She remains loyal to Osmond, however, living out her life of promise with a man she has grown to loathe.

A bright and beautiful friend of mine, let's call her Lauren, who happens to be a celebrity, and who is far more worldly than Henry James's fictional heroine, once conceded: "Put me in a roomful of good men and, invariably, I will make a beeline for the one lounge lizard in the group." Though it was stated with good humor, the observation was deadly accurate, because this classy woman repeatedly embarked on relationships with unsavory types. Only after some serious work on herself and a personal commitment to change did my friend eventually alter this debilitating pattern. The payoff? She now resides with a prince of a man.

Why, then, do we stubbornly shun valuable advice about men with poor track records, unstable romantic histories, and questionable modes of behavior? After all, we listen to advice in matters of far less consequence. Let us assume, for example, that you want to locate a specific household accessory—a certain kind of desk lamp, perhaps, or a special brand of kitchen knife. If someone told you where you might go to find it, as well as which stores to avoid, you no doubt would act on the suggestion and appreciate the advice. The person guiding you would have saved you time and energy, and with a minimum of effort, you would have secured the item and answered your needs. Why do we show less respect for the satisfying of our emotional needs? Why do we settle for the half-life of nowhere relationships?

Part of the explanation may reside in the very roots of female sexuality. In preparation for an article for the *New York Times Magazine*, Lois Gould interviewed fifty women, asking them which scenes in literature and the arts were most sexually stimulating to them. The most frequently cited references were scenes from American films in which men were depicted as the dominant, and sometimes callous, gatekeepers of feminine emotions—Clark Gable carrying a resistant Vivien Leigh up the stairs in *Gone with the Wind*, for example, or Barbra Streisand wistfully grazing Robert

Redford's cheek as this man who once dumped her lies sleeping beside her in *The Way We Were.*

What this points to, says Gould—and many therapists concur—is that some degree of masochism is a component of female sexuality. This notion has been adamantly repudiated by feminists, who argue that what gets labeled as female masochism—the desire to be sexually swept away, for example—should be viewed more accurately as women ceding sexual control to men so as not to appear unfeminine. Whatever your beliefs about the reasons some women relinquish power in their love lives, the fact remains that they frequently end up with Nowhere Men and suffer because of it. The remedy, says Gould, is for women to develop more positive self-images and to become more sensitized to the impulses shaping their romantic behavior.

One way to become more sensitized is to familiarize yourself with the many categories of Nowhere Men who inhabit the planet and who so easily divert good women from their marital path.

The Broken Man

The Broken Man suffers from some particular ill—drug addiction, or perhaps chronic unemployment—and comes with limitations that many single women seem only too happy to accommodate. A woman who is drawn to this species is a savior who falls in love with a man's potential. She plans to fix him, much as she might repair a washing machine that is on the blink.

The woman in this scenario believes that her Broken Man needs only a little understanding and encouragement to get himself back on track. Of course, he has no intention of getting a grip, since his current status is usually a lifestyle choice, not an isolated patch of bad luck. The woman in this case believes in her Broken Man more than he ever will believe in himself; predictably, the more she presses him to move beyond his problems, the more forcefully he digs in his heels.

A client, Gwen, related some of the details of her troubling relationship with just such a Broken Man. They had a whirlwind autumn courtship and were living together by New Year's Eve. A struggling actor who worked part-time as a waiter, this man spent his days attending classes to perfect his craft and going to endless rounds of auditions. But though periodically he was offered small roles in feature films or television productions, he complained bitterly that they were all beneath him. He accepted the work grudgingly; frequently, he turned down the role altogether.

With her support, he quit his job at the restaurant to spend full-time on his acting endeavors. Thus it was that she sped off to her job as a publicist each morning, leaving him in a luxury condo to read the theatrical trade papers and field offers that would be their collective salvation. But while she worked hard, he often loafed. Still, Gwen remained his ardent fan, promoting him publicly and praising him in private, certain that he would surely make his mark any day now. But the more Gwen believed in him, the more angry he became, blaming her for not doing more to foster his talent.

By the time Gwen came to see me, she had begun to worry that her Broken Man, while talented, had no intention of allowing himself to succeed. For whatever reason, he was his own worst enemy. She ended the relationship soon thereafter.

A variation on the Broken Man is revealed in another client's personal story. Roxanne was a young widow and the mother of a ten-year-old child. As a schoolteacher, Roxanne had little money in her budget for extras, and she lived a very modest, cautious lifestyle. Since money was an issue, she did not have the financial freedom to hire baby-sitters and depended on family and friends to pitch in occasionally to give her time off from her mothering duties.

Added to this mix, Roxanne also was sexually involved with a man she described as smart, sexy, and funny—and who, she assumed, was seeing other women besides her. Reluctantly, she admitted that he was probably unmarriage-able, since he drank too much and lacked financial stability. To her credit, she refused to carry on with him under her own roof and in the presence of her child, which meant that she customarily spent time with this man at his home.

Here, then, was a woman seeking marriage yet involved with a man she herself defined as unmarriageable; here was a woman with limited financial resources and almost no free time to pursue a personal life who was squandering what lit-tle time she did have on a Nowhere Man. She knew what she needed to do, but she did not want to hear my assessment: Drop this guy and use the open slots in your schedule for social activities with appropriate men. It took Roxanne many months to finally disengage, to accept that this man was never going to move beyond his self-imposed limitations or view her as anything but a convenient casual sex partner. Once Roxanne gave up her dead-end involvement with a Broken Man, her mood lifted and she watched her social world expand accordingly.

The Crybaby

One of the more annoying versions of the Nowhere Man is the Crybaby, a needy, immature whiner masquerading as a sensitive New Age male. On the surface he appears to have a laudable capacity for emotional expression and soulful responsiveness; however, soon enough these qualities turn out to be closer to melodramatic posturing, self-centered-ness, and a fear of adult responsibility. This man is less inter-ested in finding solutions to his dilemmas than in securing a willing audience for his complaints. He enjoys perpetuating his problems, which get him attention (however negative), and which shield him from having to compete on a more adult playing field.

My cousin Victoria once dated just such a man, who happened to be a physician. Fourteen years her senior, he was nice-looking and engaging but a chronic whiner. Accompany him to a special-occasion restaurant featuring fine food, good service, a pleasant atmosphere, and fun din-ing companions, and he would fixate on the disappointing berry pie. Let him have a workday in which a number of positive things happened, and he would do an in-depth monologue about the one thing that went wrong. Asking him how he was doing was always a risky proposition, since he could easily launch into an entertaining but enervating diatribe on The End of Civilization As We Know It. One could not help but feel a certain affection for this guy, but at the same time, one often wanted to strangle him. To be sure, it would be senseless for a woman ever to take the guy too seriously.

It was no accident that this man chose to be involved with a much younger woman. From Victoria's less worldly vantage point, he could appear manly and powerful without his actually having to grow up. Indeed, as Victoria matured and developed her own self-confident style, she became bored by his negativity and inertia, and she ended the rela-tionship.

The Reluctant Adult

A close relative of the Crybaby is the man whom psychologist Toni Grant, in *Being a Woman,* calls "the Eternal Boy"—a variation of "the Perpetual Adolescent" described by psychologists Connell Cowan and Melvyn Kinder in *Smart Women, Foolish Choices.* The primary fear of such boyish men is entrapment. These experts agree that this breed can become a good mate—but only if one is willing to wait patiently for him to grow into adulthood! Pushing such a candidate into marriage will only hasten his flight, giving him ample excuse to blame you for pressuring him too hard. The recommended strategy for this thorny type is to give him time to bond with you on his own, suppressing your inclination to nurture and guide him.

While I know of a few relationships that successfully evolved in this way, I frankly take a dim view of them. Women over age 35 who wish to marry do not have time to invest in a man on the off-chance that, tended and watered like a small houseplant, he might eventually grow to be a tall and commanding shade tree. Contrary to popular belief, maintaining your distance and playing hard-to-get won't do any good with this sort of man. Indeed, those tactics give him exactly what he wants: more time to escape commitment! If you must offer such a sapling a chance to flourish, make certain up front that you give yourself a concrete, internal deadline—months, not years—by which time you require a marital commitment. Then stick to it!

The Phony Manipulator

A more seriously flawed Nowhere Man comes in the form of a Phony Manipulator camouflaged as a wounded bird. This breed capitalizes on a past hurt from which he claims to be suffering—an abusive childhood, a failed marriage, or some other formative life event. Using a legitimate grievance from the past as a blanket excuse for disreputable behavior in the present, he achieves his sense of importance and mastery by making other people jump through hoops. He blames his unfortunate personal history for his inability to make a marital commitment. But, shrewdly, he leaves a woman with the impression that with just a little special handling, he might well be able to rise above his background and make a commitment to her! At first glance, this man seems sensitive and open to personal growth, but in reality he is a supremely clever actor.

Rachel, a 36-year-old friend, was involved with a textbook example of a Phony Manipulator. He was a well-heeled, never-married bachelor just shy of 40. His mother's suicide when he was in his early 20s had dealt him a traumatic blow; understandably, this tragic occurrence gave him ample reason for a heavy heart. But he routinely exploited it, melodramatically relating the story of his mother's demise and clearly enjoying its effect on the listener.

Rachel had not been successful in securing a marital commitment from this man, who danced around the issue while simultaneously pretending that any day now—if she didn't push too hard, if she played her cards right—he might be able to move beyond his suffering and marry her. He was masterful at manipulating her feminine emotions, a typical example of which Rachel recounted to me: They had spent a very romantic weekend at his place, more concentrated hours of togetherness than they had ever shared. That Sunday afternoon, as they lazily read the newspaper and sunbathed on his terrace, Rachel took the opportunity to reintroduce the subject of marriage, which they had discussed and tabled several months earlier. Once again, he skirted the subject, saying he was not ready and implying that their best chance for a future was for her to back off.

When they later went into the apartment, he said he wanted to show her something and proceeded to open a drawer from which he withdrew a velvet-lined jewelry box. "What should I do with my mother's rings?" he asked disingenuously, pointing to a dazzling diamond solitaire and wedding band set. Believing that this might be a back-handed proposal, Rachel answered in earnest by saying he should give the rings to the woman he loves. To this, he merely gave her a warning look that echoed his prior admonishment that she drop the subject of marriage. His display of the family jewels had been nothing but a mind game, an opportunity to make him feel powerful while he played her for a fool.

Rachel was a grounded woman who knew that she was being toyed with and who reluctantly decided that she must extricate herself from this manipulative Nowhere Man. She was hooked on him, sexually and emotionally, but she was also a disciplined person who wanted a psychologically healthy marriage partner. She mustered her courage and stopped seeing this man soon after. She eventually married someone capable of reciprocating her affections.

The Dangerous Misfit

Other women find themselves repeatedly drawn to a genre of Nowhere Man one could term the Dangerous Misfit. Often his dangerous side is merely a pose, but he is always an outsider whom women view as misunderstood. Heathcliff direct from central casting in *Wuthering Heights*, or, in contemporary terms, Sean Penn at his bad-boy worst, the Dangerous Misfit can take the form of the brooding poet who lives in the upstairs garret, the dark loner in the corner at a crowded cocktail party, or the mysterious stranger who repeatedly crosses your path at the hardware store. A man of few words, he does not need to explain himself, since women are more than happy to assign him a complete back-story in which he shines as a romantic hero.

I recall having a brief crush on just such a Dangerous Misfit, named Lawrence, when I was much younger. Tall, handsome, and pessimistic about the human condition, Lawrence wrote naturalistic short fiction and edited an edgy countercultural magazine known for pushing the boundaries of language and eroticism. Since Lawrence was uncomfortable in conventional social situations, spending time with him usually meant spending time in isolation. After three or four dates, I had to admit that Lawrence and I had little in common and that he actually bored me. He ended up marrying a troubled woman who had once been an exotic dancer with a drug habit—a slice of personal information he seemed almost to boast about to others.

No amount of understanding or patience will ever transform Dangerous Misfits into mainstream partners. They inhabit the fringe of society because that is where they are comfortable, and any woman seeking a long-term relationship with such a Dangerous Misfit had best enjoy living on the outskirts, too.

The Dancer

The Dancer, yet another incarnation of the Nowhere Man, has some traits in common with the Phony Manipulator. True, the Dancer's past does not include a catchall excuse for his current behavior, nor do his actions signal malicious intent. Yet like the Phony Manipulator, the Dancer performs an artfully choreographed rendition of "Come here, go away." This man never fully commits—to the next date, let alone to marriage—and since he can never count on his own feelings from day to day, you can never quite count on him. His withholding nature notwithstanding, he gives a woman a taste of his total devotion. But like the proverbial Chinese meal, he soon leaves her hungry for more.

My former boyfriend to whom I referred in Chapter Four—the man who always needed to keep his options open—was a Dancer, and I believe he probably would admit to being one. A more subtle example of a Dancer was the man who visited a good deal of grief on my client Maura, a 30-something nurse. Maura and Daniel had been conducting a long-distance relationship for more than a year. While he had flirted with commitment a number of times in his life, Daniel had never made it to the altar. Despite the built-in geographic restrictions of their courtship, Maura had catered to this man's need for "space" in other ways as well. His commitment to her seemed to wax and wane with his mood of the moment, and, consequently, she never knew precisely where she stood. Contrary to the predictions of her friends, Maura eventually persuaded him to become engaged to her.

To mark the occasion, she invited him to join her in her town, to meet more of her friends—specifically those affiliated with her synagogue, a community of people with whom she was very close. It was the custom of the synagogue that an engaged couple sponsor a get-together in the social hall following worship services—a simple affair offering a light, casual buffet lunch for the congregation. Though the fiancé was a solid professional who earned as much as or more than Maura, he had balked at the notion of splitting the cost of the event with his intended bride. Daniel's objection was not a religious one—they were of the same faith. Rather, he objected to entertaining people "he did not know"; it was not important to him, even though it was very meaningful to her that he participate.

Maura was distressed by her fiancé's attitude. On a gut level, she did not respect his response, which struck her as "cheap" and lacking grace. But her desire for marriage was so keen that she tried to accept his behavior rather than deal with the fact that she and he had divergent expectations.

Gradually, it became apparent that these two people had fundamental philosophical differences about a great many issues. Her fiancé *was* cheap, and his stingy spirit extended beyond money. He tended to withhold his time, feelings, and demonstrative affection as well. Later, this Dancer admitted to Maura that he had cold feet about the engagement. Being true to his miserly nature, he had inadvertently stumbled on a convenient obstacle to block the forward march of events. These two people soon went their separate ways.

The Casanova

A variety of Nowhere Man whom women spot easily and yet do little to protect themselves against is the Casanova. This man loves women in general so much—or, therapists might argue, hates them so much—that every woman becomes an obligatory Everest to climb. Without discrimination, Casanovas are compelled to make anyone in a skirt fall in love with them, moving along to the next conquest just as soon as the deed has been consummated.

My girlfriend Tracy was once engaged to a relentless Casanova, Ray, whose promiscuousness was apparent to everyone but his fiancée, who conveniently looked the other way. Tracy might well have ended up the disappointed wife of this cad had not circumstances conspired to throw the truth in her face just weeks before the wedding: While my friend sat in a hair stylist's chair, awaiting a haircut, she overheard the woman in the next seat telling another hair-dresser about a secret affair she was having with Ray. Tracy was devastated. Wet hair flying, she ran out of the shop and proceeded to break off her engagement.

From the female perspective, bagging a Casanova means attaching oneself to an ideal. The faulty logic goes: "If this prize catch loves me and actually commits, then I must be truly special." The problem with Casanovas is that their mar-ital commitments, if made at all, never last long. They may not divorce you, but you can rest assured that you will soon be sharing your husband with a crowd. "So many women to bed, so little time" is the operative motto, and for the undis-criminating woman involved with this type of Nowhere Man, there is virtually no upside.

The Married Man

The Married Man rarely leaves his wife for you—and if he does, he may well cheat on *you* next time around. These fac-tors alone qualify him for Nowhere Man status. A female acquaintance, involved with a married man for several years, asked my advice about how to get her personal life back on track. She complained that she had been trying to separate from him but that he kept calling anyway, and she used this fact as justification for having failed to end the relationship. Yes, I replied, he keeps calling, but you keep picking up the phone! She knew that she was never going to have a future with this man, but she was unwilling to take the courageous step of severing the tie. Instead, she used any excuse to continue along the same self-destructive course. Not until this man's wife became pregnant with their third child did the girlfriend call it quits. By that time, she hated herself for having hung in so long and for allowing the "decision" to have been made for her.

I know another woman, Annette, a young attorney, who encouraged an older man with whom she worked to leave his marriage after they had a three-month secret love affair. But while he bodily left the marriage, his spirit remained with his ex-wife. Indeed, several years into his marriage to Annette, he approached his ex with the notion of reconciling, but by that time she no longer wished to have him back. Annette might have retained her position had not the husband resented her for luring him away from wife number one. To compensate, he began a string of affairs—a skill he had honed with Annette's help.

The Abuser

Topical in the media today is the subject of the batterer, an extreme form of the Abuser, a type of Nowhere Man whom some women find difficult to leave. A woman stays in an untenable, physically battering relationship because "I love him," or because "He says he will change." Or a woman stays because she is too frightened to leave, believing the often quoted—but poorly documented—pronouncement that a woman is more likely to be killed by her abuser once she has left him.

Clearly, this is not the forum in which to argue the case, or to provide an in-depth discussion of abusive behavior, which has been well-chronicled elsewhere. But to exclude battering partners from this roundup of Nowhere Men would be equally shortsighted. Suffice it to say that under no circumstances should a woman remain with a physically abusive man, no matter how she rationalizes her choice to stay.

But a man does not need to hit you to qualify as an Abuser. He can be emotionally abusive and assault you with words. A man who consistently puts you down or demeans you, tries to make you feel unworthy, tells you what a failure you are, or blames you for all his problems is emotionally abusive. If he needs to tear you down to feel okay about himself, he does not deserve your love and devotion.

The Criminal

Finally, there exists the admittedly less ubiquitous Nowhere Man who falls into the "Convicted Felon Serving Time for Murder" category. A recently aired segment of a tabloid television show highlighted this kind of Nowhere Man with alarming precision. Entitled "Death Row Romeo," the piece featured two middle-aged women recounting their tales of romantic woe. Unbeknownst to each other, each woman had been wooed—and bilked of her life savings—by a nine-time murderer awaiting execution in a Florida prison.

Subsequent investigation revealed that over the years, the convict had preyed on twenty-six such women in similar fashion—advertising for love in supermarket tabloid newspapers and flattering the women via romantic letters from prison. Soon he controlled their bank accounts as well as their heartstrings. Describing her after-the-fact sentiments, one of the deceived subjects lamented, "It just destroyed all my trust in men." Of course, the obvious question is why this woman had been so foolish as to place her trust in a convicted murderer!

* * *

Whatever their individual labels, none of these Nowhere Men offers anything of lasting value to a marriage-minded woman. To avoid being alone, some women deceive themselves into thinking that they can scope out greener pastures without actually having to give up their dead-end guys. But rare is the woman capable of compartmentalizing in this fashion. More commonly, the woman in one of these relationships finds that her own life has stopped moving forward, while her limited Nowhere Man continues to control the interaction on his terms. The best day in a relationship with a Nowhere Man is the day a savvy woman walks away from him. Only then does she maximize her opportunity to achieve the stable and loving marriage she deserves.

Are You Involved with a Nowhere Man?

If you suspect you may be involved with a Nowhere Man—or if you have been vulnerable to such men in the past—test yourself by contemplating the following scenarios:

He may be a Nowhere Man if:

- You constantly find yourself making excuses to yourself and to others for his bad behavior.

- You feel worse after having seen him than you did before (though you try not to think of it this way!).

- He can only do things for you that dovetail with his own needs. He is incapable of doing something just because it pleases you.

- He borrows money that he doesn't pay back.

- He changes jobs often and still doesn't know what he wants to be when he grows up.

- He hates his mother and makes it the primary topic of conversation.

- He can't make commitments.

- He is jealous of your relationship with your children, your job, you name it.

- He's sleeping with you but sees you only once a week.

- He's sleeping with you but reserves his weekends for someone—or something—else.

- He's sleeping with you but you wake up alone.

- You find yourself making all the compromises in the relationship.

- He complains a lot about his ex-wife and they've been divorced for 16 years.

- You feel more like his mother or his baby-sitter than his partner.

- He has chronic problems—drugs, alcohol, unstable work history—that he blames completely on conditions outside himself.

- He says he loves you but wants to change the very things you most like about yourself.

- He keeps you on tenterhooks, never quite making a commitment or fully pulling away, and he blames you for his ambivalence (you push too hard).

- He does nothing to curb his attraction to other women while in your company—he flirts with everyone from waitresses to houseguests—and you suspect he's unfaithful when you are not around.

- He's married and says he has a terrible relationship with his wife; however, he's taking her and their kids on a two-week Mediterranean cruise.

- He's 51, has never been married, and turns green when the subject comes up.

- He keeps photos of his ex-wife or ex-girlfriend on display and still carries a torch.

- He tells lies easily and often.

- He sees himself as a victim and rejects your efforts to help him out of his rut.

- He's a taker, and his greatest sensitivity is to himself.

If you would like to rid yourself of one of these time-wasters once and for all:

- Admit that loving a man for his *potential* is nowhere.

- Understand that bad character—unlike a bad hair day—is a permanent affliction.

- Know that whatever is wrong with the relationship now will only get worse after marriage.

- Trust that if you suspect he's fooling around, you are probably right.

- Accept that no one "fixes" another person. It takes courage to lead a responsible life, and many people will cling to their weaknesses rather than work to triumph over them. In any event, the solution comes only from within.

- Believe that there *are* good, solid, marriageable men out there. You need not settle for one who isn't.

- Remember that every week wasted on a Nowhere Man is a week in which some other woman is meeting a quality, marriageable man.

- Realize that a man who really loves you should want to make you happy, and that a man for whom your happiness is a low priority is either (1) not in love with you, or (2) nowhere.

- Listen carefully and pay close attention to your early instincts about a man. Your first sense of his nature is usually the accurate one.

- Expect that a man who is somewhere should make you feel comfortable and at ease. If you are always on tenterhooks around your man—if his behavior makes you nervous or insecure—he may be nowhere.

- Attune yourself to the fact that some men are game players. Unless you are an ace manipulator yourself, be savvy and avoid this no-win type.

- Presume that if he leaves a marriage to be with you, *you* may well be the "dumpee" the next time around.

- Acknowledge to yourself that you may have had poor judgment about men in the past. You can be smarter in the future.

- Assert your intention of meeting eligible, good men. Don't pretend to be blasé about marriage and commitment. Yes, some Nowhere Men will be scared off by your forthright stance, but that is all the better, since you wish to attract only qualified candidates, anyway.

- Learn to walk away from a Nowhere Man as quickly as he would walk away from you. Lingering can only cause you pain and delay the inevitable. Act today and feel better sooner.

If you have done all these things and still find yourself involved with a Nowhere Man, do yourself a favor and get counseling. You probably need it, and you will be happier for having sought it.

A vulnerability to Nowhere Men is but one of the personal tyrants standing between mature women and their marital success. Some of the little pharaohs discussed in this and the previous chapter are so personal that people dodge talking about them altogether. Such is the case with addictions to food, alcohol, drugs—even work—that steal from us while pretending to be our best friends and that wholly undermine our chances for intimacy. The following chapter explores how.

7

Eat, Drink,
Work, Weep

A cultured divorcée in her late 40s phoned me to set up an appointment. Meredith owned a successful business downtown, and she lived in a gated suburban enclave about an hour from her office. She explained that her business (which she ran with the help of her grown children) was very demanding, that it was not the sort of environment that brought her into contact with eligible men during the workday, and that she was eager to find an appropriate mate.

As we struggled to nail down a day and time when she could make herself available for our meeting, one fact became abundantly clear: This lovely lady, who was financially secure and who had adult sons who could "mind the store," had organized her life in such a way that no one new could enter it. The perceived demands of her business functioned as a handy smoke screen, preventing her from having to forge a satisfying personal life. Think about it: Her work so consumed her that she did not even have time to see the person she had phoned for help!

For some individuals, work, food, alcohol, drugs—even cigarettes—serve as an escape from authentic living. When any activity or substance takes over one's life to such a degree that a person cannot do without it and feels powerless in the face of it, that person is addicted. An addiction puts a barricade between the individual and his or her feelings, preoccupying the person to the exclusion of other interests.

Addictions are fake friends whose dominance of one's life keeps real friends at bay. Any woman who claims to want a mate in midlife, yet who continues to be ruled by an alienating process or substance, is not being honest with herself or with others. I am not talking about moderate social drinking, or working a reasonable 45-hour week, or needing to lose 10 pounds. I am addressing those crippling romances with work, food, alcohol, and drugs that drive a wedge between a woman and her deep needs for love and affection, reinforcing her sense of isolation and helplessness. While I have empathy for these individuals, I am unable to help them with their romantic lives until they confront the graver impediments to their personal happiness; when prospective clients fall into this category, I refer them to programs such as Weight Watchers, or to relevant support groups.

At the core of an addiction lies the fear that one does not measure up. As John Bradshaw indicates in *Healing the*

Shame That Binds You, "The distorted thinking can be reduced to the belief that I'll be okay if I drink, eat, have sex, get more money, work harder, etc." As a former smoker who found every reason not to give up cigarettes, I know how serviceable such an excuse can be.

Traditional Judeo-Christian thought teaches that, if one does not believe in something beyond the self, one will put one's faith somewhere else—worshiping money, power, status, alcohol, food, or some other idol. (It is for this reason that addiction treatment programs so often link "recovery" to the patient's acceptance of a "higher power.") False gods, as it were, have the ability to seduce us, in part because our initial attraction to them begins in innocence: A woman has a vodka and tonic or eats a candy bar to soothe the stress and pain of a failing love affair, a family illness, or an unpleasant argument with a good friend. The cocktail or the sweet brings momentary relief, distancing the woman from her sadness and giving her spirits a temporary boost. Seemingly, she suffers no side effects, so each successive bout of loneliness or tension is drowned in alcohol or hot fudge. Eventually the "solution" to the problem becomes the problem itself, and the woman finds she has become an alcoholic, a pill popper, or a compulsive overeater with 40-plus pounds to shed.

Or perhaps a woman wants to prove herself at work and finds that by spending weekends at the office, she outshines everyone else at Monday morning staff meetings. She drags home the work she doesn't finish on Saturday afternoon to complete on Saturday night, providing an additional psychic bonus—a justification for her empty social calendar! What starts out as harmless conscientious behavior escalates into full-blown workaholism, which in turn generates a built-in excuse for having a dreary personal life.

Do you recognize yourself in any of these examples? If you answered yes, your addictive behavior corresponds to what some observers of our culture now call a national epidemic.

The Work God

Dennis Prager, a biblical scholar and author, and the host of a Los Angeles–based radio talk show, astutely notes that people are rarely eulogized for how hard they worked or for what they accomplished at the office. Rather, they are remembered for the kind of person they became, for the kind of son or daughter, mother or father they were. Did they make a difference in their own lives and in the lives of others? And if so, how?

Yet statistics confirm that too few of us take such truisms to heart. Indeed, the *Washington Post* reports that the numbers of hours worked by Americans has increased each year in the 1990s. This despite the fact that a national survey revealed that over half of those polled believed their workloads and job expectations to be "excessive," and a full one-quarter said they had "no time for family." Perhaps these findings clarify why Workaholics Anonymous, a twelve-step program patterned on the same principles as Alcoholics Anonymous, now has over seventy chapters in the United States and about a dozen in other parts of the world.

Once a predominantly male affliction, workaholism today is gender-neutral. And as the authors of *Women and Self-esteem* point out, the stereotype of the unmarried woman who works a 70-hour week, dresses like a man, and speaks in sports metaphors is but one incarnation of the female workaholic. She is also "the waitress who hangs around the restaurant after her shift is over . . . helping out as much as possible, because when she takes her uniform off, she feels a loss of identity." And "the secretary who goes in early and stays late without compensation just to make sure she's done the job right." And the production assistant who gives up a well-deserved and much-needed vacation to cater to the caprices of her self-centered boss. Sadly, the list of examples is endless. And in each case, the addicted woman forfeits the opportunity to enrich her life beyond her office walls.

While the drawbacks to such blind attachment to one's work may seem obvious, the potential benefits are more difficult to decipher. What does the work smoke screen do for the woman who builds it? Apparently, a lot. It helps to numb her emotional pain, curbs her loneliness, and offers her a forum in which to continually prove self-worth and importance ("Look how much I'm needed"). It depletes energy such that she has no time left for intimacy. It offers a way for her to feel successful and admired without having found a mate. It gives her a convenient "out" for not having to risk uncomfortable social encounters. And so forth. Using work as a crutch (one that I personally leaned on for years) is often less scary than the alternative: declaring oneself emotionally available.

A healthy and vibrant enthusiasm for one's work—and a deep commitment to it—is admirable and does not a workaholic make. The issue here is totally one of degree. Does the work eclipse the rest of your life? Constitute your sole identity? Prevent you from forming intimate attachments? Clearly, economic reality dictates that most women must work. And to be certain, today's corporate downsizing and ever-spiraling cost of living force many women to work longer hours than they might wish. But among my own clientele, at least, *over*working appears to be a personal choice. Significantly, a fair percentage of these workaholics are self-employed, in occupations ranging from manicurist to management consultant; their extra hours on the job are not imposed upon them by a boss or a supervisor but are, rather, the product of their own design.

All these women work a minimum of 55 hours per week; some put in as many as 65 or 70 hours. While they universally express the desire to improve their personal lives, not one of them pursues outside activities except for work-related ones. And though they claim they want to develop new interests, few seem motivated to curtail their frenetic work schedules to achieve this goal. Initially, many of these women looked to their work to supply a sense of mastery, realizing perhaps that the world of dating and intimate relationships caused them to feel insecure, anxious, or even, incompetent. Unfortunately, the more they defined themselves through work, the less likely they were to feel confident in other spheres of their lives; their lack of satisfaction in personal relationships became a self-fulfilling prophecy.

A charming and funny friend of mine in the Midwest, Cynthia, conforms to this model. Highly trained in her field and very well compensated by her company, Cynthia typically works 55 hours during the week, spends a good portion of her weekends on business-related matters, and socializes exclusively with well-heeled people who have a connection to her profession. She was in town on business not long ago, and we ended up having a Saturday night dinner together in a restaurant dominated by romantic couples. She surveyed the room and in a moment of unusual candor wistfully remarked, "I've been a flop at finding a man—my work is the one thing I'm successful at doing." Her vulnerable statement, uttered in a little-girl-lost voice, acknowledged that her career somehow owed its luster to her impoverished personal life. I've always believed that Cynthia could have both a mate and a good job, but the choices she continues to make affirm the primacy of power and status over her other values.

My friend lives in a culture that celebrates the virtues of being a work junkie. A woman who puts in a 12-hour work-day, then swings into a restaurant booth for a business dinner looking fresh and savvy, is praised for her stamina and resilience. National magazines run feature pieces on ways to pack more activity into one's overloaded day, how to harness home-office technology, where to jump on the ubiquitous information superhighway—all these topics are geared toward maximizing productivity, not fulfillment. As previously touched on in an earlier chapter of this book, only rarely does anyone question where all this intensive rushing and "doing" get us.

Melvyn Kinder, in *Going Nowhere Fast,* sees clues to our misplaced values in the very language we use to define career progress. We are "on a fast track," he says, "climbing the corporate ladder," or perhaps "ahead of the power curve." People "on the way up" become addicted to motion. They covet the adrenaline high of working at a fevered clip; they love the "ride." Kinder observes that such individuals often begin to deceive themselves about the personal price they are paying, and that this heavy toll includes losing touch with their emotional and spiritual potential as well as their sense of self-worth.

I recall being mesmerized by motion when I worked as an executive in the entertainment business some years ago. At that time, I typically put in 75-hour workweeks and had the heady, giddy delusion that I was indispensable. A cross-country flight on a red-eye to make an important New York meeting, the sexiness of being "on the road," the urgency of connecting with a particular writer or director before another studio beat me to it—this visceral, physical rush constituted a primary payoff.

While I lived in this fantasy world, I had no time to sustain a personal life. My weekends, when in town, consisted of wading through an endless stack of screenplays—few of them well written. I remember a particular Sunday when my boyfriend at the time suggested a nice romantic walk on the beach, which was only five minutes from my front door, but I said I was too busy to take time out for it. Had I been performing intricate brain surgery, this would have been a reasonable excuse. Under the circumstances, my response verged on the pathetic.

Several years later, I made a conscious decision to leave my gilded corporate cage, largely because I suspected that I would never sustain a lasting relationship leading to marriage unless I changed the way I was living. Indeed, by paring down my lifestyle and shifting its emphasis, I laid the groundwork for meeting my special man.

For people such as I at that time, the breaks between assignments—the spaces separating the demands of work—can be terrifying. These people dread being alone and in a noncrisis mode, and they invariably find ways to complicate their lives so that they do not have to confront the void. I once worked with an unmarried workaholic who begrudged anyone who took time off—especially for, excuse the expression, a "family" vacation. She made certain that her calendar was always filled with obligations—most of them work-related. This woman so feared being alone that she would frequently double-book her lunch and dinner engagements. This allowed her to plug up the holes caused by last-minute cancellations. She seemed to need nonstop movement to prove that she was actually alive. Or perhaps, as

Melvyn Kinder notes of classic workaholics, her well-being was "measured by momentum and achievement, not inner peace."

The high-powered, workaholic management consultant played by Diane Keaton in *Baby Boom* slows down only when the demands of the baby she "inherits" force her to experience the pleasures of "being" rather than "doing." When the demands and pleasures of motherhood begin to divert the energy she once reserved for her work, she finds herself out of a job. She trades her careerist existence for a pastoral life in Vermont, where she starts making homemade applesauce for her child. This hobby burgeons into a gourmet baby food business, which becomes wildly successful—poetic justice, perhaps, for the character's having followed her heart. She learns that her life has intrinsic value independent of her latest accomplishment or corporate coup. Her self-worth does not hinge on *doing* anything; it is okay simply to be.

Single women in the real world can break free of their workaholic tendencies, too. A good example is Lindsay, a woman who made time to meet with me despite the demands of her 70-hour-per-week, fast-track job at a big consulting firm. The stress of Lindsay's job was literally causing her hair to fall out. She very much wanted to find a husband, and while it sounds funny to say, it was clear that she would be bald and alone unless she slowed down and allowed some grace into her life. Eventually, she gave up her VP stripes and took a less lucrative, less taxing job in a related field that still made use of her management background—a change that gave Lindsay more time for recreation and new interests. She subsequently became engaged to a man she met while on vacation. Now that's poetic justice!

Am I Working to Live, or Living to Work?

To determine whether you qualify for workaholic status, answer the following questions, using a separate piece of paper. Do you:

1: Work more than 45 hours per week?

2: Work while you eat?

3: Work in bed when home "sick"?

4: Work on weekends and holidays?

5: Take work home when you don't need to—or take home more work than you'll ever complete?

6: Think about work when you're supposed to be having fun?

7: Have a preoccupation with time?

8: Find it hard to "do nothing"?

9: Have a hard time relaxing? Is your "free" time planned?

10: Allow work to eat up your time for exercise and recreation?

11: Make time accommodations for your boss that you wouldn't make for a friend?

12: Find you can't say no when asked to do a task, even if doing it puts you on overdrive?

13: Take overtime compensation in money rather than in extra time off?

14: Forfeit your accrued vacation time?

15: Schedule business meetings before and after business hours as well as during the business day?

16: Work social plans with friends or new men into your

schedule only at the last minute if time permits, rather than make definite plans?

17: Invent crises so you can solve them?

18: Have a reputation for being late to social and family functions?

19: Use coffee, cigarettes, or sugar to energize you—or excessive exercise, pills, or alcohol to relax you?

20: Are your work life and social relationships fused, rather than independent of each other?

21: Play (tennis, Scrabble, poker, etc.) only to win, rather than simply for the joy of playing?

22: Find yourself frequently irritable?

23: Display an intolerance for weaknesses and mistakes—in others and in yourself?

24: Begrudge people who have other priorities besides work?

25: Secretly believe that people only like you because of your job description, not because of who you are?

If you sincerely wish to marry and yet answered yes to many of these questions, you need to reorient your priorities immediately. Here are a few tips to get you started. These suggestions may not lead directly to Mr. Right's door, but they will definitely enhance your ability to find it.

1: Most workaholics are perfectionists, so begin by curbing your perfectionist thinking. As discussed in Chapter Three, this means eliminating "musts" and "shoulds" from your vocabulary and replacing them with self-praising pats on the back.

2: Start *acting* as though there is more to life than work by taking advantage of non-work-related activities. Eventually, you'll actually *believe* there is life beyond the Xerox machine.

3: Build some nonwork relaxation time into every work-day—as few as 15 or 20 minutes if that is all you can manage at first. Use this refreshment break to meditate, walk, jog, do yoga, paint, sing, bake, listen to music, take a bubble bath, read the personals. Or just sit and do nothing. The one requirement is that you empty your mind of everything related to work. Well, there is actually a second requirement: The activity you choose should be something other than watching television, which you probably do anyway and which has a tendency to numb rather than inspire.

4: Do something nice for yourself every day. Buy a new nail polish. Set a date with a friend. Read a non-work-related magazine article. Research ideas for your next vacation. Give yourself a facial. Do not let a day go by without being good to yourself in some small specific way.

5: Curb your tendency to be abrupt, irritable, or unreasonable with superiors, peers, underlings, or friends and family. When this inclination shows up, apologize to the person on the spot (a straightforward "I'm sorry I snapped at you, please forgive me" will do nicely—no need to dive into lengthy psychobabble by way of explanation).

6: Keep a portion of your weekend "work-free," much the same way that many restaurants are now smoke-free. Plan in advance which hours of the weekend will not have work bleeding into them, then be brutal about keeping those hours uncontaminated. As busy as I was during those stressful corporate years I referred to earlier, I made it a rule never to look at work-related materials before four P.M. on Saturday. This meant that I could shop, have lunch with a friend, go to the gym, or get a manicure without guilt—I had given myself permission in advance.

7: Delegate more, double-check less. If you supervise others, practice the art of surrendering control to subordinates who are more than competent to take up the slack. Then forget about it! Do not hover over the poor soul to inspect the quality of the work or the exact way it's getting done. Assume you've delegated to a responsible individual. (After all, you probably had a hand in hiring him or her, right?)

8: Start saying no to extra work when it comes your way— there will always be someone else down the line who'll be insecure enough or masochistic enough to overextend and say yes. At the very least, begin to say no to assignments that are not central to the job you were hired to do. (Resist the temptation to be swayed by managers who try to appeal to your weakness with buzzwords such as "teamwork" and "pitching in." You were hired to do a job, not to take up slack, or to do someone else's job. And if you were hired to work a 40-hour week and find you're working 50, speak up. People will not respect your limits unless you make it clear that you have some!

9: If you run your own business and realize it is running you, evaluate how you can restructure your method of operating. Consider taking in a partner, hiring more support staff, or merging your business with someone else's. Since these choices may translate into reduced profits, calculate how you might pare down your living expenses to accommodate a freer lifestyle. If you're self-employed or work freelance and do not have extra help to whom you can delegate, analyze how you can reduce your total number of work hours per week without radically altering your lifestyle. Perhaps raise your fees, for example. Or reduce the amount of time you spend on a given project. Or spend less money on the materials you use. In other words, in addition to working fewer hours, learn to work smarter.

The Food God and Other False Deities

The second section of this chapter explores other addictions that can hold sway in a woman's life, attacking her core values and her belief in the future. As you read about these addictions, honestly ask yourself whether any of the examples apply to your own experience. If they do, you alone wield the power to renounce your addictive behavior and choose healthier ways to live.

A potential client called to find out about my program, and in the space of five or six minutes she told me quite a lot about herself. There was nothing in her history that sounded like a significant factor in her singleness, until she added, as an afterthought, that she was 60 pounds overweight. (And if she was acknowledging 60, the number may well have been higher.)

To paraphrase Dr. M. Scott Peck, writing in *A World Waiting to Be Born*, addictions represent our feeble attempts to return to the Garden of Eden, to a protected and child-like state of perfect oneness with the world. By whitewashing or repudiating one's addictive status (the tactic of the overweight woman described above), a woman undermines her ability to move forward in the desert beyond Eden and become all that she can be.

It is fashionable to believe that, to cure a problem, one must understand its genesis, and that some conditions—such as obesity—derive from genetic deficiencies beyond the person's control. But the reality is that, except for what experts term the "morbidly" obese (whose condition may be metabolic), the vast majority of weight-afflicted individuals are fat because they do not have the will to eat less and to exercise more. And the vast majority of individuals who stay hooked on alcohol, drugs, or other damaging substances *remain* addicted because they have not made the commitment to face life sober.

Single women who rely upon these distorted means of coping severely limit their chances for attachments to men—except to men who themselves are addicted or who are supportive of addictive behavior. Further, psychologist Harriet Braiker, writing in *The Type-E Woman,* notes that "some women use alcohol, drugs, or food to sabotage their achievement" altogether. "Psychologically," she explains, "if you blame your drinking problem (or weight problem, etc.) for your not achieving your potential, you avoid the real issue of testing the boundaries of your talent." Thus, a woman afraid she may fail in the romantic arena stays fat, or she continues to drink to excess, so that she will have a ready-made excuse to explain why men reject her.

Joyce, a 39-year-old client who consulted me some time ago, came to see me again—this time for help in composing a personal ad to run in a local newspaper. Joyce had originally sought my advice because she had been unable to sustain a deep intimate relationship with a man, although she had dated periodically throughout her adult years. Quite simply, few of the men she went out with ever called for a second date.

I remember feeling at that time that Joyce's demeanor and attitude had the word "deprived" scrawled all over them; she greeted the world from the perspective of someone who felt cheated out of her due. But at the same time, she rejected any and all constructive ideas on how she might attempt to change her "bad luck." In fact, during our two initial meetings, she directed most of her energy toward rebutting my suggestions! Nevertheless, I sensed progress when she called about placing the personal ad; finally, she was prepared to take some action, or so I thought.

Answering Joyce's knock at the door, I tried to contain my shock: During the nine or ten months since I had last seen her, Joyce easily had gained 30 or 40 pounds—and she had not been of model proportions to begin with. She later explained that a physical ailment contributed to her changed condition, stating that her doctor said nothing really could be done. But when I probed, asking if she had obtained a second medical opinion, to verify that indeed "nothing" could be done, she reverted to her usual negative self. The extra weight, it seemed, offered her more comfort than did the prospect of slimming down.

When I encouraged Joyce to mention "full-figured" or "zaftig" as one of the ways to describe herself in her ad, she balked; if she did that, no one would respond. I tried to convince her that she was setting herself up for further rejection. While complete disclosure might translate into fewer responses, those men who *did* answer would be men who preferred larger women, and such men would be more likely to return for a second date. Not surprisingly, Joyce chose to run the ad without the suggested description, and her "bad luck" continued.

It seemed as though Joyce had begun to use food as a shield against intimacy, much as Mary Tyler Moore recalls once having used alcohol. "I had a lot of ways of anesthetizing myself against pain," Moore says of the years leading up to her treatment for alcohol dependency at the Betty Ford Center. Drinking became a form of escape, she says; soon her cocktail became her "best friend." Moore's road to recovery included learning that she could be lovable without being "perfect," an obsession that had dogged her all her life. Once she let go of the illusion that she could control everything, her life became more manageable and she was on her way to a more gratifying existence. Her new beginning eventually encompassed a new husband—a handsome, accomplished doctor many years her junior.

The Power to Change

If your own life centers on alcohol, food, or some other damaging substance, you know how often you are lying to yourself and others to perpetuate your habit. Therefore, to transform your self-indulgent, addictive lifestyle into something more valuable requires a *relentless* commitment to honesty. However, berating yourself for your damaging behavior only serves to reinforce it. As we saw in Chapter One, guilt feelings are little more than cop-outs, excuses for not committing to self-improvement or to change. So if you genuinely want to rid yourself of an addictive habit, give up the self-loathing and drop the guilt. Otherwise, your behavior will merely deteriorate further to match your sinking expectations.

Melvyn Kinder stresses that a diet or an addiction treatment program is "doomed to fail" unless the individual makes this mental adjustment and achieves a measure of self-acceptance. The compulsive overeater, the alcoholic, or the chemically dependent—like the work-addicted—can begin to change her thinking by *acting* as if she already believes herself worthy of something better. She can pass up that tempting hot fudge sundae, for example, affirming to herself that there is something better in store for her—a thinner body, more self-respect—if she curbs her impulses. Eventually her thinking will catch up to her newly improved behavior.

One of my most memorable clients, a 45-year-old woman I'll call Cheryl, came to me for advice on how to expand her social universe. She had not dated much in her life, and she needed some basic pointers on contemporary dating etiquette. When I asked Cheryl how she had changed in the last five years, she told me that, after struggling with a weight problem all her life, she had finally lost over 100 pounds. It had taken her almost three years to accomplish this; now, she was normal-sized for the first time since childhood. My admiration for this remarkably disciplined woman could not have been more profound. She had accomplished her personal transformation without the benefit of expensive medical help or a supportive network of family and friends. Average-looking and a bit of a loner, Cheryl had imagined herself worthy of a better life, and she had remade herself in that image.

What can Cheryl's story teach us about self-acceptance? "If you love yourself," offers John Bradshaw, "you're willing to delay gratification so that something else more conducive to your growth might take place." Rabbi Abraham Twerski, a medical doctor and theologian who works extensively with addicted individuals, points out that one's ability to elevate one's life in this way is the true meaning of the biblical directive "I have placed before you today life and death, the blessing and the curse." Paraphrases Twerski, "Choose life so that your dignity and humanity can endure."

The next chapter explores the last of our personal pharaohs, those unhealthy overattachments to family, friends—even pets—that can easily become life rafts to nowhere.

8

The Velvet Web: Cozy Attachments That Keep Us Single

"Leaving home will not become a reality until we stop seeing the world through our parents' eyes."

—Judith Viorst, *Necessary Losses*

In Jane Austen's classic masterpiece *Emma*, the heroine of the same name suffers from a surplus of familial love and support. The only child of a wealthy, indulgent widower father, Emma basks in the protection and security her father represents, and she confides that she has no motivation to seek a life beyond his approving gaze. Even when Emma falls in love with an old family friend, Mr. Knightley, she cannot imagine marrying him if doing so will disrupt her father's comfort and routine. Accordingly, Mr. Knightley moves into Emma's father's home after the wedding, allowing her now to minister to the needs of both men at once!

The solution to Emma's dilemma, while wholly acceptable in Jane Austen's day, strikes the contemporary American imagination as being ill-advised, perhaps even a little weird. Yet a surprising number of today's midlife singles marginalize their opportunities for marriage by staying locked in just such intricate dances with parents, siblings, children, former spouses, friends—even pets. The needs and attentions of these "substitute mates" may fill a woman's dance card, but they only intermittently blunt her loneliness.

To be sure, some responsibilities particular to one's middle years cannot, and should not, be avoided: Aging parents may become increasingly dependent, requiring more of one's time and energy; growing children, if one has them, continue to need nurturance and a structure they can count on; ex-spouses who are the fathers of one's children must be reckoned with on matters relating to the family's welfare; and so forth. However, problems can begin when a woman starts appropriating other people's lives and pretends they are her own life.

We've all seen examples of these contaminating connections. Take, for instance, the bookkeeper who uses her parents and their friends as her chief social outlet, spending what little free time she has with senior citizens rather than with her peers. Or the professional woman, long separated from her husband, who does not get a divorce but instead keeps him in her life as her buddy/confidant, delaying the hour when one or the other of them will move on. More extreme perhaps, but not uncommon, is the example of someone like my former hair stylist, a long-divorced 47-year-old who takes her Schnauzer to her salon, uses him as a traveling companion, and in fact turns down weekend invitations if they require leaving him behind. Predictably, this animal has an anthropomorphic name, Fred. In essence, the hair stylist is living a dog's life.

Forging an Independent Life

A midlife single who becomes so enmeshed in the lives of others may discover that her opportunities for marriage, or remarriage, have slowly faded under the glare of a borrowed sun. Unless a woman remains alert to the pitfalls of her enveloping attachments, these relationships can easily grab hold of her for good.

While I was completing the manuscript for this book, my husband and I became parents for the first time. As I now watch our infant daughter's fantastic voyage of self-discovery—her charmed absorption with her own hands, or a ceiling fan, or a shaft of light—I am reminded of our solemn task: to make her feel secure and loved in such measure that one day she'll be independent enough to leave us. If we have done our job well, or at least well enough, this will be the result. It is the desired outcome, since only as a separate, autonomous being will she experience a rich and effective relationship with the world and with herself.

When parents fail to foster such competence and autonomy in their children—or when adult children refuse to disengage from their families as a way of avoiding or postponing responsibility—everyone loses. For the single woman whose connection to her well-meaning parents or to her dependent adult children is excessive or emotionally invasive, the results can be stunting. You may recognize yourself as the weak-willed adult child or as the overinvolved parent in this scenario. In either case, your family ties may be inhibiting you from moving on in your own life, which includes the meeting of new eligible men and the pursuit of marriage.

Writer Judith Viorst describes the realization that growing up means pulling away as one of our "necessary losses"—one of life's emotional hurdles that we conquer in order to mature and flourish. But not everyone makes this transition a reality, says Viorst; some people get stuck. Maggie Scarf, author of *Intimate Worlds: Life Inside the Family* and an intrepid investigator of family dynamics, concedes that relationships in which family members look to one another for the satisfaction of their emotional needs are not necessarily destructive. They become injurious, however, when the connections leave people no room for air, in what Scarf calls "a state of suffocating emotional fusion." There's an old Jewish story that quite neatly captures this quality of excessive interdependence: As an elderly couple carry their adult son through the marketplace, someone stops them to commiserate about the son's inability to walk. The old couple are taken aback. "Of course he can walk," they reply, "but why should he have to?"

The family tug that keeps some of us from making a leap into our own future—or that prevents us as parents from letting go—remains complex psychological terrain. Usually, the explanation for such arrested development lies not in a single factor but in a web of interlocking factors that conspire to retard one's progress toward maturity and independence. But while the causes may seem opaque and hard to fathom, the results virtually stare us in the face.

Women who have been "overparented" easily fall prey to boredom and restlessness, for instance. Accustomed to relinquishing responsibility, they often choose expediency over challenge and risk, rarely testing their abilities or stretching themselves. I had a friend in high school, Janet, whose gluey attachment to her own mother prevented her from fully engaging in life. They appeared to be best friends as well as mother and daughter, so much so that Janet even imitated her mother's style of dressing, with matronly results.

A good student, Janet received acceptance letters from several fine colleges, and she was in the fortunate position of having parents who were financially able to send her away to school. But she did not want to leave her mother, and enrolled in a commuter college instead, choosing to live at home, where her mother continued to rinse out her nylons, as she had always done! When Janet eventually did marry, her new husband went into the retail business with her father. So in establishing her own home, Janet never really built a new nest; she just added on to the original one.

Luckily for Janet, the enmeshment with her mother did not prevent her from creating a family of her own. Rosemary, a woman with whom I consulted not long ago, fared less well. A delightful woman but socially shy, Rosemary found it "easier" to stay glued to her family, whose relationship with her she described as being a close one. Although Rosemary was "college material" and, like Janet, had parents who could afford to educate her, she did not pursue a higher education. Instead, she went to work for an accountant, with whom she stayed for more than 25 years— not as an associate or an assistant but as a receptionist. Rosemary left the job only when the 72-year-old accountant retired; with few marketable job skills, she found herself without a position or a direction. To make matters worse, while her folks had been her anchors and the focus of her world, her parents were now deceased, and Rosemary, approaching 50, experienced chilling confirmation that many of her choices—or, more accurately, her *failure* to make any significant choices—had been a mistake. In the second half of her life, Rosemary now struggles to fashion something of value for herself.

When we allow our parents to fight our battles for us, to become entwined in the minutiae of our lives, we lose confidence in our own judgment and decision-making. And when, like the adult child of the old couple in the story cited earlier, we allow ourselves to be carried long after we are able to walk, we may have trouble distinguishing between true intimacy and mock closeness.

Judith Viorst quotes a startling example of one woman's difficulty in separating her own feelings from those of her intrusive mother. In an interview, the younger woman made a statement to Viorst, then followed it with: "Now that I've said that, I'm not sure if I thought it or my mother thought it, or if I only thought that my mother would have wanted me to think it."

Such an overinvestment in a mother's opinions can make it tough to locate one's own emotional center. Recall in an earlier chapter the client who put emphasis on power and status—traits she wanted in a man. And recall also that her mother desired these values for her. The boundaries between mother and daughter were so sloppy that the single woman had trouble differentiating where her mother left off and where she began.

Sarah, the 37-year-old sister of a friend, displays a similar need for maternal validation that causes her to second-guess herself constantly. Sarah never seems to know what she thinks or feels separate and apart from her mother, a circumstance that was thrown into relief recently when Sarah fell in love with Matthew and needed her mother's stamp of approval to know whether the feelings were real. In fact, Matthew was an inappropriate choice for a number of reasons, and true to form, the mother offered her complete analysis explaining why. This is not the first time that Sarah has picked unwisely and looked to her mother's "better judgment" to set her straight, a repetitive mother/daughter dance destined to keep each woman in her respective role—and to keep Sarah single!

In some families, the requirement for harmony, togetherness, and a sole family vision eclipses the development of individual preferences and beliefs among the family members. Such ill-defined boundaries lead to a kind of groupthink, in which ideas—and by extension, people—outside the family unit never become wholly accepted. Think how hard it would be for a new man to break through such a fortress!

Over the years, I have known personally, or heard stories about, a number of single women whose backgrounds fit the description of a closed family unit—and more often than not, these women idealized their families as being better than, or preferable to, all others. In early childhood, we idealize our parents as a natural stage in our own development. But this unrealistic infantile view soon evolves into a more mature and balanced assessment. We begin to recognize our parents' shortcomings as well as their strengths, seeing them as fallible humans rather than invincible gods. If this reality check never takes place, however, we remain awed observers.

Among my former classmates, colleagues, and acquaintances, several such women come to my mind immediately—each a woman in her 30s or 40s who so idealizes her parents' marriage or family that she has not risked establishing a family unit of her own. Perhaps the fear of falling short of the mark keeps these women from finding partners. Or maybe their inflated concept of having come from such "perfect" families makes them wary of altering the delicate balance on which their security rests.

Whatever the explanation, these women never fully separate from Mom and Dad or become autonomous adults. So complete is their identification with their parents' lives that these women often describe their personal feelings and experiences in terms of the plural "we." Although there may be a certain comfort in such a collective existence while one's parents live and thrive, there may be much turmoil and regret to contend with later on.

The Trap of the Daddy's Girl

According to experts in child development, it is the father even more than the mother who is the vehicle through which a girl arrives at an idea of her worth, both as an effective person in the outside world and as an attractive, desirable woman in relation to men. A girl whose father validates her in these arenas grows up to be a self-confident and competent woman. And if, in the natural course of things, the father encourages his daughter's independence from him during adolescence, she is able to move forward gracefully and ultimately to establish healthy intimate attachments with other men. However, if the father's involvement in his daughter's life is so intense that the girl's closest bond is with him rather than with her mother, she easily becomes what is called a Daddy's Girl. In return for his generous nurturance of her, the father of a Daddy's Girl is respected and adored.

The glitch in this system occurs if the father does not let go, in which case the daughter never leaves him psychologically. Remaining attached to one's father in this fashion breeds unrealistic expectations of other men, since no one can possibly measure up to the heroic dimensions of the idealized parent. A Daddy's Girl who has not made the appropriate break from him often experiences the normal expectations of an intimate relationship as excessive and unfair compared to the unconditional love and favor of her overly devoted dad.

Among the women I have known both personally and professionally, the Daddy's Girls who never detached carry a heavy load. Some of these women remain single today, never having found men who could match their all-powerful fathers. Of the women who did marry, many divorced, often reporting that their husbands could not fulfill their emotional needs.

If you have never married, contemplate whether an overinvestment in your father has colored your ability to appreciate other men. Is it possible that no other man has been allowed to measure up to the larger-than-life image you cart around with you? If you have been married in the past, you might ponder whether an excessive attachment to your father—or to his thinking and expectations—cast a pall on your relationship. Were your demands of a former husband unrealistic, given his own nature and strengths? Was it easy to find fault and almost impossible to praise? Did you pick a weak man who would never compete with your father, and then resent him for not commanding your respect?

A Daddy's Girl who truly wants to marry must move beyond the bounds of her private Oz. She may recognize that she is in a rut, and that her prior expectations of men have been unrealistic and exclusionary, but her misperception need not be a lifelong affliction. The sooner she adjusts her father's pedestal and stops discounting worthy men, the more content she will be.

The Caretaker

Sometimes overparenting, or our excessive reliance on the goodies it brings, leads us to feel we owe our parents something. They have given us so much, surely we are responsible for their happiness and must be available to them always. Or we believe we must achieve to please them. Or we submerge our negative emotions and true feelings to avoid disappointing them. The consequences of these mental contortions? We get lost in the perceived expectations of our parents and limit our ability to set out on a path of our own.

Celia's story carries many of these components. I met this down-to-earth, never-married 45-year-old a few years ago through a volunteer organization to which we both belonged. One of the first things I remember about Celia is her attachment to her parents, whom she described in glowing terms. They had been Holocaust survivors and had made a new life for themselves in this country after the war. But while Celia admired her parents enormously, she also saw them as controlling; they had strong opinions about what was, and was not, acceptable, and their opinions influenced her greatly.

Celia regretted the absence of a husband in her life and implied that she had never married because she had not wanted to abandon her parents. She felt protective toward them, while at the same time fearing their judgments. Though her parents lived some 400 miles away and had no physical infirmities, Celia visited them an average of two weekends per month. Since she worked full-time during the week, this meant that her schedule afforded almost no time for meeting new eligible men.

To complicate matters further, Celia lived with a male roommate, a platonic friend whose presence on the scene provided welcome company and made her feel safe. Didn't his presence inhibit would-be suitors as well? I asked. Or at minimum, temper her motivation to seek male companionship elsewhere? While Celia viewed her male roommate as being no social-life deterrent whatsoever, I tended to disagree. America's favorite sitcom characters may reside coed at age 24 and not necessarily betray any particular emotional bias—but choosing to live coed at age 45? To me, this seemed a pretty clear statement of Celia's ambivalent attitude toward intimacy. Interestingly, Celia described her male roommate as being "just like family." Her roommate filled up the space an eligible man might have filled. Her selection of him seemed designed as an insurance policy against her marrying and deserting the parents whom she felt were so dependent on her.

Sooner or later, the woman who compulsively caters to everyone else's needs (as a way of not thinking about her own) ends up feeling angry and resentful. So says psychologist Harriet Braiker in *The Type-E Woman*. This occurs, says Braiker, even though the woman herself sets this imbalance in motion.

Sometimes the perceived expectations of family consume all our waking moments, as evidenced by Donelle, the younger of two daughters in a family she characterized as being perfection itself. Donelle, a never-married woman in her mid-40s, consulted with me because she wanted to find a mate. Almost immediately, however, this claim proved in conflict with Donelle's idealized picture of her parents' marriage and her unrealistic conviction that her parents would fall apart without her.

When I first met Donelle, she had recently moved into her parents' home, back into her "old room." She explained that neither parent was in the best of health and they needed her to look after them. While Donelle did not make a huge salary, she earned a good living as the office manager for a big law firm—enough to afford a lovely apartment of her own, a medium-priced, late-model car, and a nice wardrobe. She asserted that, contrary to what I had assumed, her parents were financially comfortable. Why, then, had Donelle not hired a temporary helper to perform some of the household chores and caretaking so that her own life would not be thrown so completely into chaos? After all, she already had the responsibility of a full-time job and a demanding schedule. Since she lived in the same community as her parents, she would still have been able to see them whenever she wished. While Donelle agreed that this could have been an alternate solution to the dilemma, in her mind it was not as satisfactory as moving home and rendering the help herself.

Donelle told me that her previous relationships with men had always hit the wall because she had too much of a need to be needed, and therefore she picked overly dependent men. Even her job description—office management—denoted a woman bent on organizing and easing the lives of others. Donelle could have selected an alternate mode of behavior; at a minimum, she could have balanced her compulsive giving with respectable amounts of attention paid to herself. But apparently she found it easier to continue repeating the past. While she may have harbored some vague fantasy of herself as a married woman, she feared it more. There had never been a divorce in Donelle's "perfect" family; what would happen if she failed? Donelle's decision to devote herself so exclusively to her parents' care thus served a protective purpose, too. As long as they needed her, she avoided having to risk a valid, independent attachment to an eligible man. If a woman such as Donelle is sincere about wanting to marry, she must face her fears and change her lifestyle, or her dreams will remain hollow illusions.

The Good Mother

Too much of a good thing is not a good thing, an adage that more than applies in Gail Sheehey's penetrating look at midlife patterns and behaviors, *New Passages*. Sheehey distinguishes a current phenomenon among the young adult children of people in their middle years: In part because of narrowing economic opportunity, the younger generation is delaying its move into adulthood, postponing its financial and emotional independence.

Sheehey astutely notes that the growing trend of young adult children to continue living at home plays right into the hands of divorced and widowed women weary of the dating scene. The presence of an adult son at home fills the emotional and physical space formerly reserved for a mate. In like manner, the adult daughter easily becomes a mate replacement, someone with whom the unattached woman shares confidences and socializes, and toward whom she looks for affirmations of love she isn't getting elsewhere in her life. Sheehey calls these seemingly harmless relationships "lethal social contracts" because they hinder both mother and child from pursuing intimate attachments beyond the family fold.

One of my friends has a former sorority sister whose experience bears witness to Sheehey's assertion. I had heard a lot about Leeann before I actually met her. She was supposedly a vivacious and attractive 50-year-old divorcée who wanted to remarry but had not been having much success in her personal life. Since my friend had always described

Leeann as being enormously outgoing and upbeat, I was curious to find out why such a woman would be in a social holding pattern.

Leeann had a variety of interests and hobbies, largely centered around outdoor activities such as sailing, bike riding, and tennis; she had a good job to which she devoted about 45 hours per week and which afforded her some money for "extras"; her children were grown and out of the house; and she was in excellent physical condition because of her passion for exercise and people-oriented sports. What was wrong with this picture? Why was this woman not meeting new marriageable men?

The answer lay in Leeann's tight connection to her unmarried 28-year-old daughter, who lived nearby. In her daughter, Leeann had a best friend/confidante, a readily available buddy with whom she enjoyed cultural events, weekend trips, and Saturday night forays to coffee houses and singles hangouts. Such easy access to companionship dulled any incentive for either mother or daughter to move beyond the comfort of the familiar and to venture out on her own. Then, too, Leeann's youthful spirit and her apparent desire to defy her biological age by associating with a younger crowd meant that the social situations in which she landed exposed her to men half her age! Had she actually been looking for a "boy" friend, this could have been a bonanza, but she said she wanted a mature, established mate.

Leeann's amiable relationship with her former husband, from whom she had been divorced a number of years, proved to be a comparable liability. While she honestly had no wish to be his wife again or to have a sexual relationship with him, clearly she liked having him in her life. Accordingly, he joined her and the "kids" for holidays, family outings, and celebrations, and even accompanied

Leeann on spur-of-the-moment bike rides, or to the occasional movie. Since her ex-husband lived nearby (did you doubt it?), and since he had never remarried either, his attachment to Leeann and their adult children remained primary.

Given this much reinforcement of the past, is it any wonder that Leeann's romantic life had gone nowhere? Consistent with all the other factors, her most important relationship outside her family unit had been with a no-strings younger lover, a man whose position in her life would never upset her exquisite family tableau. Unless she examined her motives more closely, of course, Leeann would never grow beyond the boundaries she herself had defined.

The Friend in Need

In Leeann's case, the impediments to marriage happened to be familial. But staying glued to one's friends of both sexes can also reduce the chances of meeting new men, as well as quell the motivation to circulate. I plead guilty to this particular offense, which no doubt prolonged my own tenure as a single woman.

During the years in which I held a corporate job, I juggled a demanding schedule full of social obligations, most of them in some way related to my work. Since I was not involved in a serious committed relationship for much of this period, I often needed suitable escorts to accompany me to dinners, screenings, barbecues, holiday parties, and—the most dreaded of all invitations when you're over 35 and single—weddings.

Fortunately, I had two unattached male friends who were only too happy to squire me around town and who took turns being the man on deck. One of these men, a good listener and someone who genuinely loved women, had been twice married and divorced. Long ago having determined that marriage was not one of the things he did well, he candidly shunned any suggestion that he reenlist. The second male friend—handsome, charming, and a good sport when asked to show up in a tuxedo—was gay. Since each of these men fit easily into almost any social situation, and since they were my pals, not "dates" as such, I felt free to relax in their company.

What I did not factor into this equation, however, was that having such available escorts at my side constituted a mixed blessing. If I truly wished to find a mate (and at the time, I *thought* I did), I was squandering countless opportunities to bring new men into my circle. True, it would have made for a less predictable evening had I invited my newly single dentist or that former classmate from my high school reunion to be my banquet date. But taking such minirisks could have shaken things up a bit—perhaps even led to a serious relationship—while playing it safe was never going to bring me closer to the altar.

Surprisingly perhaps, the pitfalls of relying on convenient male escorts pale by comparison to the limitations that result from our attachments to our dearly beloved female friends—those alter egos whose natures and sympathies so mirror our own that we would marry *them* if only they were men! (I of course refer to your optimistic, supportive, loving girlfriends, not those male-bashing whiners with axes to grind whom we discussed in an earlier chapter.)

Female friendships are integral to my life, as they may be to yours. My women friends have been cherished sources of love and support always. What possible downside could exist in such a bond? In short, our female friends accept us so unconditionally that, in their company, we can escape having to work on ourselves. While in our younger years our female friends may nourish and sustain us through good times and bad, and sometimes even stand in for men during fallow dating seasons, by midlife, these loyal, accepting comrades often supplant men altogether.

Without even realizing it, we begin to lean on our female friends to provide the steady companionship that otherwise might be reserved for a mate. Outwardly self-sufficient and content, we stick together in bunches while sending out an unconscious signal that we do not need men at all. I can think of several clusters of single female friends whose cliquishness sends out this very message. Women who move in packs such as these put themselves at a decided social disadvantage, because no man wants to run a gauntlet of females to strike up a chat with one of them. Furthermore, relying on one's female friends for stimulation and company saps one's initiative; why bother making a social effort with strangers, one might reason, when complete love and acceptance are so close at hand?

It would be comforting to believe that our single female friends can be the source of fix-ups and introductions to new men, and in our earlier years, this may well have been the case. But by age 35 or so, our friends' lives have often become as insular as our own. Chances are we've already *met* all their single male friends. And if none of us is having experiences beyond our tight-knit social circle, how will any of us have access to fresh marital prospects?

My intention here is not to demean the female friendships that I, for one, value so deeply. Rather, I am suggesting that we too readily use these relationships as a substitute for taking social risks that could bring us into contact with eligible men and possibly enrich the quality of our lives. The lazy or timid may not wish to hear this, but socializing on your own rather than in the company of your female friends enhances your marital prospects. If you go to a party or other event solo, you force yourself into more interactions with other guests than would likely occur if you had companions to lean on. Then, too, arriving stag makes an unambiguous statement to the other guests: "I am unattached, I am available." Therefore, unencumbered men will find you highly approachable, and other people's dates will receive some free advertising about your potential availability for the future. Even if you do not actually meet any new single men on such outings, you may well make other new friends who themselves become potential sources of introductions to eligible prospects.

Woman's Best Friend

At the risk of seeming to equate human companions with members of the animal kingdom, let me now say a word or two about pets. A previous chapter suggested the possibility that dogs and cats—or less conventional creatures, such as guinea pigs, should one have them—can usurp the time, attention, and bed space otherwise occupied by a real live man. Rare is the woman who actually prefers the company of a canine to that of *Homo sapiens*, but devoted pets make us feel needed and loved; furthermore, in the absence of a mate, a pet can help to fill a void.

On the downside, a relationship with a pet that begins as pleasant compensation can also evolve into a limiting lifestyle, if one isn't careful. The correction here does not entail abandoning your rottweiler or your regal Siamese but putting its primacy into perspective. If you claim to want to get married but use the care and feeding of your pet as an excuse for passing up activities with two-legged animals, you have a problem. Adjust accordingly. And if you are going to spend a certain amount of time on the care and maintenance of a pet, by all means let this responsibility enhance your social life. Walk your rottweiler in parks or on jogging paths frequented by men, for example, or enter your Siamese in well-attended cat shows.

Redrawing Our Boundaries

To wean oneself of cozy attachments requires vigilance in the extreme. If you have been part of an enmeshed relationship, no doubt it evolved over a long period of time; therefore, you can hardly expect to redraw your boundaries overnight. The mandate is not that you should stop talking to your mother, or turn your back on your adult children, or ditch your best friend, or give away your precious border collie. Appropriate remedies lie in the healthy exercise of new muscles, not in the radical amputation of viable limbs.

We need a safe place in which to express fears and vulnerabilities as well as to celebrate triumphs and achievements; a haven in which we are accepted for our true selves, at our worst as well as our best; an environment that nourishes us spiritually, emotionally, intellectually, and physically. Parents, no matter how devoted or accommodating, eventually must leave us; children, if we've raised them right, leave us, too. The alternate nuclear family represented by our friends can only go so far in providing the sustenance and support, the challenges and the personal growth that we would otherwise derive from a loving committed relationship with a mate. And pets, despite their many attributes, cannot fix a garbage disposal, dance the cowboy cha-cha, or take us to dinner.

In the truest sense, married or single, we all wake up alone. But in partnership with an appropriate companion, that aloneness often melts by virtue of its proximity to a warming kindred spirit. Rebekah, whose biblical story unfolds in the book of Genesis, marries Isaac, a virtual stranger, and goes to live with him far away in the land of Canaan, leaving behind her parents, and siblings, and all she knows. She does this because she has been told that she has a greater destiny to fulfill beyond the confines of her family's walls. Indeed, in striking out on her own, Rebekah eventually becomes one of the four matriarchs of the Bible, a role model for womankind.

The modern single woman who moves beyond her own little world may be less exalted than Rebekah but no less courageous. If she is committed, focused, and clear, aware of the self-inflicted obstacles to love, and ready for success, a whole new world awaits her. How to access that world is the subject of Part III.

Part 3

Match Point: How to Win the Game

9

Change Equals Opportunity

Sharon (in her 40s) met Louis at a charity auction. She had gone to this event under duress—she had not had a chance to wash her hair, and she was wiped out after a long day at the office. What Sharon really wanted to do was to curl up with the new *People* magazine and a bowl of Ben & Jerry's Chunky Monkey ice cream. Yet she was also feeling somewhat guilty because she was committed to this particular charitable cause and had as yet done nothing to support it.

Louis happened to be in her town on business and had come to the auction as a way of filling a free evening. The two of them ended up bidding on the same inexpensive trinket, and when the loser congratulated the winner, a match was made. Had Sharon given in to comfort and stayed home that night, she and Louis never would have met.

Angela (in her 50s) met Jack because of her passion for the Green Bay Packers. A woman who occasionally treated herself to weekend getaways, Angela landed at a country bed-and-breakfast during the height of the football season. The inn had no television, and, eager not to miss the Sunday Packers game, Angela asked the proprietor whether he had any friends who might be watching. No problem, came the reply.

Within 20 minutes, Angela had arrived at the home of strangers and was installed in their den, watching the game along with a roomful of their friends. Jack, of course, was one of the friends, and the rest, as they say, is history. Angela's willingness to put herself in a potentially uncomfortable situation—in a roomful of strangers—altered the course of her life.

Hannah (in her 40s) met Marty at a religious service sponsored by a synagogue to which neither of them belonged. They worked in unrelated fields and lived in communities 30 miles apart. They had no friends in common. When Hannah and Marty eventually tied the knot, they chose as the site of the nuptials the place that had brought them together. Had Hannah not gone to an unfamiliar environment where she was unaffiliated, she would not have met her man.

I happen to know all these people personally. In fact, the Hannah/Marty story is my own. What unites the three of us women in the examples cited is that we were all involved in activities outside our normal spheres of movement—we had extended ourselves beyond our customary boundaries. And in so doing, we brought magic into our lives. Note that the activities that opened the doors to marriage in these cases were not singles events (more about such events later in this chapter). We three women were merely going about our lives in creative ways, doing interesting things we had never done before, in the company of people we had never met.

To gain perspective on just how many new experiences you typically have within an average week, make two copies of the Time Management Chart shown on **page 176.** (The chart, a seven-day calendar in grid form, can be drawn using unlined 8½-by-11-inch paper and a ruler.) Using your datebook or calendar for reference, fill in one Time Management Chart, accounting for each segment of each day over the course of a full week. Pick a week from the very recent past, preferably the week that just ended. Indicate where you were for each time period (breakfast, mid-morning, lunch, mid-afternoon, dinner, evening), what you did, and with whom. Write down even those activities that may seem too insignificant to mention. For example, if you ate dinner alone while watching television, write that in. If your mid-morning was spent on errands or in a boring meeting with your supervisor, indicate that in the appropriate slot. And so forth. Be thorough and honest. It is the only way this exercise will work for you.

Now be a harsh critic of your own habits, behaviors, and desires for familiarity and comfort. How much of your activity was redundant? Did you eat many meals alone at home? If you ate out a great deal, did you go to the same one or two places you always go? When you went to work, did you travel the same route you usually take? When you socialized, did you see the people you generally see? Are certain patterns emerging? Circle them clearly. Now circle all the activities, people, and places that you were exposed to for the very first time that week. If you can't find much to circle here, you are not alone.

Time Management Chart

	Monday	Tuesday	Wednesday	Thursday	Friday	Saturday	Sunday
Breakfast							
AM							
Lunch							
PM							
Dinner							
Evening							

The Time Management Chart you just completed graphically indicates that when you stick to your old ways of doing things, the same old things keep happening to you. Yet you bought this book precisely because you want to change what has been happening!

Your weekly schedule need never appear so uninspired again—not if you commit to a new course of action. To that end, paste a duplicate of the Time Management Chart on your bathroom mirror or another surface that you are certain to see daily without fail. Now, using miniature Post-its that you label, plot out one new experience that you are going to have for each of the seven days of the week.

For example, if you usually eat breakfast at home alone, commit to having your coffee and bran muffin in a public café or popular breakfast spot at least once a week—ideally, in different cafés in different neighborhoods, no repeaters for a while. Label the Post-its with the café names and affix them to the breakfast slots in the appropriate columns. If breakfast out is not in your budget, eat at home first, then stop at the café for coffee only. Or bring your muffin *with* you—it's not against the law! If you are not comfortable eating in public places alone, a phobia we discussed in an earlier chapter, "get over it," as a famous Eagles' song admonishes. (Remember, the three women whose stories opened this chapter met their eventual mates while they were out in the world by themselves, not traveling in a pack.)

Shake up your routine. Do something new . . . or do something old in a new way every day. Ask yourself each morning what you are going to do that day/that week in the service of your personal life. Add it to your Time Management Chart. Then do it. The new experience can be as daring as a flying lesson or as pedestrian (literally) as walking a new

Time Management Chart

	Monday	Tuesday	Wednesday	Thursday	Friday	Saturday	Sunday
Breakfast				7:30 Walk on San Vicente path 8:15 Breakfast Starbucks		8:30 Walk on San Vicente path 9:15 Breakfast Paris Cafe	
AM	Call Charlie R. and David S. re: intros to new Men. Call Lisa B to follow up re: intro to her cousin, Al						
Lunch							
PM			Call synagogues to get on mailing lists			4:30–6:30 opening reception Renaissance Art Gallery	2:00–3:00 Work in booth at Starlight Foundation Fund-raising Fair
Dinner							
Evening		Edit draft of 1st quarter status report, plus pay bills, at Public Library			8:00 Services and social at Beth-El synagogue		

route to the office. Lest you imagine yourself in a state of perpetual motion, consider this: Very often, the new experience for the day will not be an activity at all, but rather a phone call, an inquiry, or a bit of research regarding an activity or event you'd like to pursue at a later date. To get an idea of what a well-developed Time Management Chart might look like, see the sample on **page 178**.

At the end of each full week, you will pull off the old Post-its and begin to develop a new set of goals for the coming week. The crucial element of this new approach to life is proactivity. Doing more for your personal life makes you feel good. Feeling good makes you more attractive and approachable. Being more attractive and approachable draws more new people and new experiences into your sphere. There are no shortcuts to this logical domino effect, but its viability is borne out by the countless numbers of women whose marital "luck" changed when they altered their habits and routines.

Expanding Your Social Universe

So now you are on the train. You have placed your Time Management Chart in a prominent spot, ready to be filled in. Your miniature Post-its are close at hand. But you are ready to do what, exactly?

The Master List that follows highlights strategies, ideas, events, activities, organizations, and institutions that can bring new experiences and, therefore, new people into your orbit. The selections are designed to enlarge your social universe, not specifically to bring a prince to your door. The old adage proffered by a generation of mothers, "Through people you meet people," actually has merit. Keep in mind that since it's just as easy for you to meet a potential mate through new married friends as it is through a singles club, it's shortsighted to turn up your nose at a particular suggestion simply because it involves spending time with the already hitched.

Not every idea on this Master List is for everyone. Consider the list a smorgasbord from which to choose what appeals to you personally. If you're susceptible to motion sickness, or hate what the wind does to your hair, or live more than an hour from a body of water, for instance, chances are that boating and sailing won't be for you. Similarly, if you still cringe from the memory of having read your original composition aloud to the fourth-grade class, you may not wish to sign up for a creative writing seminar. But it's a big wide world out there; the choices of how you experience new things and meet new people are restricted only by the amount of time you invest and by the limits of your own imagination.

Master List

Churches and Synagogues

I placed this entry first because it is one of the options that single women often consider last. By visiting churches and synagogues, I do not mean a woman should undertake a multidenominational sweep of every religious institution, or that she should pick one congregation and affiliate with it exclusively for the rest of her natural life.

Joining one congregation works well once one has formed a family unit, but it is no way to find a spouse. When considering this option: (1) identify a number of houses of worship that roughly correspond to your beliefs (even if you'd normally say "that's not for me"); (2) call the administrative office of each house of worship and get on its mailing list—tell them you are interested in finding a new congregation and would appreciate receiving their bulletin of upcoming events; and (3) begin to circulate among the various congregations.

The important ingredient is to circulate, rather than to choose the momentary warmth and comfort of one church or synagogue. While singles events are always worth sampling, it may be far more productive to attend events that draw the congregation at large—not only the regular services, but also lectures, concerts, charity auctions, and so forth. If you have young children, select some events that include families, since there are bound to be a few single fathers in the bunch. Bear in mind that married couples— particularly the husbands, when pressed into service—can be excellent sources of future introductions to other men. So make it your business to meet all kinds of new people, not just that lone single guy in the back row.

In addition to bringing a single woman into contact with new men, houses of worship offer the obvious benefit of spiritual renewal. Whether one comes from the position of believer or skeptic, exposure to a meditative environment— a stimulating sermon, or beautiful music, or a chapel whose architecture inspires higher thoughts—can be nourishing and restorative. There is no downside to spending your time in this manner, since you are sure to come away with *something* of value.

The Rolodex Role

Returning to the adage that through people you meet people, realize that everyone you know can be a resource for fix-ups. Buy yourself a purse-size spiral notebook and divide the pages into two columns. In the left-hand column, enter the names and phone numbers of everyone you know who could be the source of introductions to new men. This includes not just your good friends and relatives—and their spouses, who should be listed separately—but everyone you know casually. Included in the latter group would be your doctor, dentist, pharmacist, clergyman, stockbroker, contractor, accountant, hair stylist, manicurist, neighbors, and so forth. To make sure you leave no one out, compose this list while leafing through your personal address book and your office Rolodex.

Now begin calling everyone on this list—a few names each day until everyone has been called. (The calls qualify as the "something new" you have done that particular day in the service of your personal life; they should be entered on a Post-it and stuck on your Time Management Chart.) Explain that you very much want to meet new men, that only through friends and acquaintances can a woman hope to meet quality people (flattery encourages compliance!), and that you're sure he or she can come up with one good name for you. This assignment will probably be uncomfortable at first, since it involves exposing your sincere feelings and laying them on the line. But the exercise gets easier with each successive phone call, especially when you remind yourself that your purpose has merit and that there is nothing wrong with wanting to meet eligible men. Be quick to remind those you speak with that you are an adult and take full responsibility for what happens after the introduction has been made (men in particular tend to worry that they'll be held accountable for another man's potential bad behavior).

If one of your resource people seems resistant to the idea of helping you, do not lose sleep over it. Graciously thank him or her for listening and move on to another, more productive call. If you are hesitant about asking coworkers or business contacts to be part of your introduction brigade—a legitimate concern—consider whether some of these people might become appropriate resources for you at a later date (after a particular work project has been completed, after a sale or presentation has been made, and so forth). It is far easier to turn a business relationship into a personal one after the specific business purpose has been achieved. However, there will always be certain professional contacts with whom you'll never wish to cross this line, and you should honor your instincts in this regard.

People who work should be called at their offices, during the day, since this is where they're accustomed to doing serious thinking. Men are the best sources for knowing other men, so do not leave out the spouses of your female friends. Present the challenge in a lighthearted way; if a man says, "Gee, I can't think of anyone off the top of my head," tell him, "David, I just know there's got to be one appropriate guy stuck in your Rolodex between the K's and the T's." Then jog David's memory by running down the list of possible suspects—coworkers and former coworkers, clients and business contacts, former fraternity brothers, doctors, dentist, CPA, racquetball or poker buddies, insurance broker, and so forth.

Once David comes up with a name—and if you've been an adorable pest, he will—write that new man's name next to David's name in your spiral notebook. Indicate the date of your conversation with David, who has now promised to call Hank, his recently divorced chiropractor, on your behalf. If you do not hear back from David after a week or two, it's imperative that you call him again. Do not talk yourself out of following up. People are busy with their own lives; your dating needs do not occupy center stage for them, so you must nudge the subject back into their consciousness.

Continuing to assert your desire to be introduced to new eligible men—and following up on all leads—maximizes your chances for marriage. You need not feel embarrassed or out of line. The one caveat is that each situation must be judged on its own terms. For example, if David keeps stalling about making that introduction to Hank, it's possible that he's trying to spare your feelings by avoiding telling you that Hank isn't interested in a fix-up. If you suspect that such extenuating circumstances exist, don't nag. Instead, let David off the hook and suggest that perhaps he can think of another candidate who would be a more realistic choice. Do reciprocate to those friends and acquaintances who come through for you—a personal note will do nicely, unless you've been a colossal pain or you've met Mr. Right, in which case flowers are de rigueur.

Art Galleries and Museums

Get your name on gallery mailing lists by personally calling each gallery and asking to receive announcements about, and invitations to, upcoming shows. Gallery events are almost always free and attract an interesting crowd. You'll even get wine and cheese along with the watercolors. These gatherings do not require that you commit to an entire evening; most receptions occur during the cocktail hour or on weekend afternoons. Nor do you need to know anything about art to enjoy the shows. Use your lack of knowledge as a good conversation opener with a stranger. "I'm not familiar with Reicher's work," you confess in a confidential tone as you eyeball an oversized canvas in black acrylic, "is he always this somber?" (This gambit works as long as the person you are talking to is not the artist!)

Museums, too, prove fertile environments in which to

meet new men. In addition to exhibition areas, most museums have lecture and film offerings, as well as a restaurant or a coffee shop. Again, get on the mailing list so that you'll be informed about upcoming events well in advance.

If your budget allows, you should also consider becoming an active supporter of the institution. At a certain level of giving, which varies according to the particular museum, supporters receive invitations to special parties and activities organized specifically for them. These gatherings expose you to a range of people you probably would not otherwise meet. If you work for a large company or corporation, your employer may have a program that offers matching funds for any nonprofit contributions you make. In that case, whatever money you donate to the museum could be matched by your company—a terrific way for you to get involved for half-price, so to speak. And, of course, at year's end, your portion of the contribution would be tax deductible on your personal income tax form—as if you needed any further encouragement!

Charity and Volunteer Work

The personal and societal benefits to involving yourself in some form of charity or pro bono work were noted in an earlier chapter of this book. There is no substitute for old-fashioned volunteerism to temper self-absorption and make us feel valuable.

Since you would like to meet eligible men while you make your contribution to society, pick your arena of service wisely. Someone may need to coordinate that weekday morning rummage sale to benefit the Salvation Army, for instance, but that someone need not be you. You want to volunteer your time during the evening or on weekends, when men are more likely to participate.

As previously mentioned, if envelope-stuffing and stamp-licking do not grab you, you can find more demanding areas in which to make a contribution. Most nonprofit organizations welcome whatever special skill or knowledge a volunteer brings to the table. Organizations that can use your input range from children's and medical charities to environmental action groups, literacy programs, and homeless shelters.

Political Campaigns

On the local, state, and national levels, political campaigns offer a world of possibilities to the enthusiastic volunteer. Do not expect to be given the kid-glove treatment here, however. These fast-paced environments excite and engross, but they rarely coddle the hardworking volunteer staff. However, if you're energetic, eager to work, and not too thin-skinned, you can have a great time attaching yourself to a political race. If you know something about advertising, finance, communications, publicity, computer graphics, or the like, be sure to ask to be assigned to a particular task. Call the local headquarters of the party of your choice to find out how you can get involved.

Adult Education Classes

Whether you wish to learn basic photography, conversational French, Eastern religious thought, or ballroom dancing, there is an adult education class somewhere for you. To find out where, call the local college or university in your area. Speak with the department of continuing education, or adult education, and request that a catalogue of the next semester's courses be sent to you. Generally, you do not need a college degree to take these courses, nor does taking them earn you credit toward a degree.

In addition to courses offered through academic institutions, additional classes can be found through organizations such as the Learning Annex, should there be one in your city, or local community centers. Be sure to choose subject matter that has some appeal to men. You are taking the course because it genuinely interests you, yes, but remember, you'd also like to get married! A class in textile making, Chinese cooking, or nineteenth-century romantic poetry has little chance of producing eligible candidates. More fruitful outcomes might be expected in classes relating to less rarefied subjects such as financial planning, sales and marketing techniques, public speaking, political science, computer applications, and so forth.

Give a Class

If you have a field of expertise, or an artistic hobby, or a special physical skill, consider teaching a class in it. You may have a special talent that you take for granted but that others would benefit from knowing more about. Sharing what you know in this fashion builds confidence while it exposes you to new people.

To find out where you might be able to offer your services, check out course catalogues from local adult education programs and community center programs, as well as from the Learning Annex, if your city has one. In addition, familiarize yourself with the types of classes offered by churches, synagogues, and service organizations in your area. To get a feel for how such classes are taught, enroll in one yourself (as suggested earlier in this chapter). If you don't see your particular topic offered in an existing class, contact the program coordinator by phone and follow up with a written proposal outlining the course material you wish to teach. After some initial jitters—which are only natural—you might find you like being in front of a class. People who are otherwise shy in public-speaking situations sometimes discover that they practically forget about the audience when they are teaching something they love.

Getting Physical

Activities that require some physical exertion have the dual advantage of improving your body shape and mental outlook while bringing you into contact with other vital people, some of whom are bound to be single men. A gym or health club offers obvious possibilities. Pick a large, centrally located gym that draws a varied and sizable clientele.

Gyms have rate schedules that are almost always negotiable. Do not talk yourself out of joining because of cost. Do not get all dolled up to go pump your iron, either. Heavily mascaraed women, dripping in gold jewelry, look foolish panting on the Stairmaster, since it's clear what's weighing them down! Do take the time to look clean, attractive, and nicely attired in workout clothing that flatters your assets and minimizes your flaws. If you have a nice waist, for instance, but your legs could be sold to Steinway, don't wear an oversized T-shirt and shorts. Divert attention from your lower half by wearing black stirrup leggings that give you a long slim line, and highlight that Scarlett O'Hara middle with a belt or a torso-hugging top. As always, wear age-appropriate clothing, not paraphernalia designed for the MTV crowd.

Busy, *employed* men—and let's face it, those are the ones you want to meet—exercise in the early morning, after five P.M., and on the weekends. Plan your workout schedule accordingly. There may be a wait for the treadmill at these peak hours, but this down time encourages social contact with your fellow calorie-burners. And, instead of rushing home to pop a frozen Weight Watchers Spicy Penne with Ricotta dinner into the microwave, stick around the food court and see what develops.

If you do not play golf, tennis, or some other social sport, now is the time to learn. If you already play but are rusty, now is the time to get back in gear. Introductory lessons in a group clinic atmosphere are the best way to get going—you need not feel self-conscious there, since everyone starts from the same approximate place. These lessons usually can be found at nominal cost at public or high school courts, or at a public golf course or driving range. Private golf and tennis clubs sometimes offer lessons to nonmembers, too. No matter where you take lessons, once you gain some rudimentary comfort with the sport, the facility more than likely will be able to arrange games for you with others of similar ability.

Again, don't run to your car or hop the bus the minute the lesson is over. Buy a lemonade at the snack bar, pull up a chair, and watch the other players, or ask some questions of the friendly pro who just taught you how to lob. The casual clubhouse setting makes conversation easy, since you can always talk about the sport that brought you there. Don't squander this social opportunity by being in a hurry. To where exactly are you running?

Hiking and Biking

In most cities, the Sierra Club and other outdoor adventure organizations offer a range of organized activities for hiking and biking enthusiasts. Check the Yellow Pages of your phone book, or the listings in your local city magazine, if your city has one.

Jogging and Walking

Most cities have special jogging and walking paths favored by people who pursue such activities. These popular routes, which draw an eclectic group of people, can be non-threatening and invigorating environments in which to meet other health-conscious individuals. Even if you have to drive 10 or 15 minutes to get to such a place, it is well worth your time. After all, you'd drive that far to see a mediocre movie or to shop at the mall. And this is free!

Cafés, Coffee Houses, Diners, Outdoor Restaurants

Casual dining establishments provide excellent opportunities for social interaction. Scope out the popular watering holes in your area—such as the breakfast spots I referred to earlier in this chapter—and make it your business to spend time there. If you have young children at home, this suggestion probably will not fit into your schedule. If, however, you have no one who depends on you at mealtimes, you have no excuse. You need to eat anyway; why stay cooped up at home or at your desk at work when you could be in the company of others?

If you are self-conscious about eating alone in public, take a book, magazine, or newspaper for company. If you freelance or work from home, take your work with you and feed your professional and personal lives at the same time. And don't pick a table all the way in the back, next to the bathrooms and the exit sign. The point is to see and be seen, not to blend into the woodwork.

Public Parks

Public parks provide many of the same opportunities for social interaction as do casual eating establishments.

Obviously, parks can be used for all manner of physical activity. But, in good weather, the park is a place where you can also eat your lunch, read the newspaper, walk your dog, do your work, compose on your laptop computer, and, unless it is very windy, pay bills, too. Countless chores that you might otherwise relegate to the solitary confinement of your kitchen or home office can actually be accomplished in public. And many onerous jobs—such as balancing your checkbook or finishing a status report for your department head—become far less daunting when addressed out in the open air, with the sun shining down on you and the possibility of someone wonderful crossing your path at any moment.

Seminars in Fields Other Than Your Own

This idea works most effectively for the single woman who has some flexibility in her daily schedule and some discretionary income. Many professions offer half-day or full-day seminars, often with breakfast or lunch included, for people in fields ranging from law, medicine, and finance, to architecture, entertainment, and high-tech electronics. I am not advising that you spend time and money listening to panel discussions on integrated circuitry. But if you are a curious person in general, there is certainly some new arena you'd like to know more about.

I suggest that a single woman expose herself to topics and professions outside her own field of endeavor because sticking with people who do the same thing you do can become an insular proposition. This is not to say that you shouldn't also attend seminars and classes to broaden your knowledge of your own field—this is always a good idea. But the advantage of professional events in fields other than your own is that they expose you to a roomful—or in some cases, a ballroom full—of professionals you'd never otherwise meet, and roughly half of these professionals probably will be men. That is, unless you picked fashion, nursing, or education as the new field you'd like to know more about, in which case, pick again.

Advertisements for these specialty seminars can be found in professional and trade journals, not in your morning newspaper. Visit the periodicals section of the public library and ask to see these publications. If the event you'd like to attend is open only to people with credentials in the given field, call the event coordinator and request that an exception be made for you. Speak with confidence. If the field you've chosen actually relates to the work you already do, explain this fact. If you are new to the field, explain that it is one you are considering studying or writing about. A slight variation on the truth, in this case, hurts no one, and you may actually find a new career along with an eligible man!

The Public Library

In the course of writing this book, I spent countless hours at the public library. Had I been single at the time, I might well have found a mate, too, because the place attracted some very appealing men of various sizes, shapes, and ethnic persuasions.

Pick a library branch in a well-traveled part of town, and use the branch as a work environment, much as you would the other venues listed earlier. Except for the "no eating or drinking allowed" policy, all other endeavors can be carried out there. If you prefer a man who still goes to work every day, then lunchtime, evening hours, and weekends provide the most possibilities. However, if a retired person suits you as well, then any weekday morning will do. Find a comfortable chair in either the current periodicals section or the main reference area and get to work. You may or may not meet an eligible man this way, but at a minimum, your professional and personal chores will get done, freeing you for other activities on this Master List.

Chambers of Commerce

Most chambers of commerce have organized activities—breakfasts, speakers, and so forth—for the businesspeople in their city. For a fee, one can become a member, and one need not be a corporate mogul to join. The groups draw their membership from regular working people who care about networking, civic concerns, and local business opportunities. And since these groups traditionally have attracted more men than women, the male-to-female ratio at chamber events tends to favor us—what a refreshing change! Remember that married men can be an excellent source of introductions to unmarried men, so don't get depressed just because you see a lot of wedding rings. If your local chamber is poorly organized and does not offer regular events, volunteer to organize one.

A Word About Singles Events

I confess to having painful memories of the few singles dances I attended over the years. Invariably awkward affairs, these functions featured an excess of overdressed middle-aged women in hot pursuit of the few men who had shown up. The dances looked more like high school mixers than adult gatherings. Such a lopsided showing does little for a woman's morale.

That said, some women swear by such events. I know a lively woman in her 50s who volunteered to be the coordinator of a professionally oriented singles group. Some months into her tenure, she saw a handsome new man from across the room at one of the dances she had organized. Since she had official duties at the dance, she had a built-in reason to approach him and make him feel welcome. He turned out to be a retired judge and widower, a very fine man with a marvelous sense of humor and a real desire for a committed relationship. Knowing a good man when she saw one, she wasted no time cutting him away from the herd. They married shortly thereafter.

This woman's story notwithstanding, the best kinds of singles events are not dances but activities that offer an educational, cultural, professional, athletic, or religious experience along with the exposure to eligible people. This eliminates the "meat market" effect of the typical singles dance, and allows you to come away from an event or activity with *something* valuable, even if it is not someone's phone number. Singles activities that fall into this category range from concerts, progressive dinners, and hikes, to ski trips and religious retreats.

To find out what your city offers in the way of organized singles activities, review all those church or synagogue bulletins you're now receiving; check out the singles or personals sections of the daily newspaper and of specialty or neighborhood newspapers; and read the display advertising in the personals section of your city magazine, if your city has one.

Dating Services

Dating services can be viable methods for meeting eligible men, but the quantity and caliber of the men very much depend on the service. I personally know several happily married, well-matched couples who met through a nationally recognized dating service. Remember that fees for these

services vary widely and that published fees are always negotiable; don't pay an excessive price just because it is written
in a brochure or on a service contract.

A large dating service whose members select one
another via self-composed biographies and personalized
videos should be willing to let you browse through its member books before joining, to satisfy yourself that there
indeed exist the types and numbers of men you'd want to
meet. A smaller service should be willing to share data
about its clientele, as well as supply references from satisfied
female clients. It may well refuse the latter request, but you
really have no other way of ascertaining the truthfulness of
its claims. And tell the service so.

Matchmaking Services

The variety and quality of these services vary widely. You
may know that some nationally advertised services have
been discredited in recent years, and therefore healthy
skepticism must prevail. I'm sorry to report that I know few
satisfied customers of professional matchmakers. This is a
shame, since the principle of being introduced by a third
party, who theoretically has gotten to know the man and the
woman in question, is a very good one. My advice on this
subject is: Invest in a matchmaker only if the individual's
integrity and track record can be verified by someone you
know and trust.

Personal Ads

Over the course of my single years, I periodically "played
the personals," so to speak, and found them to be a fun and
productive way to meet eligible men. At times when my
social life might have been experiencing a particularly dry
patch, I could answer or place an ad and suddenly create a

flurry of activity where previously none had existed. If nothing else, this buoyed my spirits and reminded me that there *were* eligible men out there, and that one day I'd find my match.

My most memorable "personals" date occurred six or seven years ago with a man whose magazine advertisement made him sound fascinating: an educated, solvent, 40-something owner of a business in a creative field, he listed exotic travel, gourmet cooking, fine dining, reading, tennis, horseback riding, and antiquing as among his numerous interests. A real Renaissance Man, he had said of himself. Sign me up! I dashed off a response letter and sent it to him, together with a flattering but not doctored black-and-white head shot of myself. My Renaissance Man called soon thereafter, and we set a date. The restaurant of my choice, he had said.

Nothing could have prepared me for what happened the night of our appointed date, as a humongous white stretch limousine tried unsuccessfully to round the corner of the small street on which I lived. As my curious neighbors flocked together to discuss what was up, I tried to slink away unnoticed. Okay, I thought to myself, as I receded into a plush bucket seat whose leather still smelled from the factory, so he's a little showy and over-the-top. Maybe he's a nice guy anyway.

As the evening progressed, there were more embarrassments—all centered on this man's relentless ego and need for attention. Yes, he knew a lot about a lot of things—so much so that he entertained himself with his many talents and had no desire to be complemented by anyone else's strengths. He wanted an audience, not a partner.

But along with this unsuitable man, I had other more promising experiences with men I met through the personals. In fact, I can think of one man in particular who could have been a serious contender. Unfortunately, I met him while I was still mourning the loss of one of those Nowhere Men we discussed in an earlier chapter, and I was unable to appreciate the gem glistening before me. How blind!

In the last few years, the use of personal ads as a vehicle for meeting new men has come under attack, because of mounting fears about exposing oneself to unsavory or dangerous individuals. While I would be far more cautious today than I was in less chaotic times, I would still use the personals if I were single. However, very strict safety rules should apply (and will be discussed shortly).

Clients always ask whether it is better to place ads or to respond to them, and my answer is: Do both. If you simultaneously place ads and respond to them, you maximize your chances to meet the largest selection of eligible men. Remember that the type of publication you use may determine the type of man you attract. An upscale city magazine or a professional journal most likely caters to the more educated, sophisticated man; an arts and entertainment–oriented newspaper may draw a more creative though sometimes less solvent readership. And a local newspaper may tend to attract a very broad spectrum of candidates, from working-class men to high-powered professionals—however, this venue is less selective and more chancy, to my way of thinking.

Most personals sections allow the respondent to answer by phone or by letter. Whenever possible, use the mail. For reasons of safety, rent a post office box and use it as your return address on all correspondence. If you have placed the ad, receiving a note by mail allows you to find out more about a man than you'd ever glean from a message left on your answering machine. If he's handwritten his response, you get to see his penmanship—erratic handwriting is a red flag, indicating that the man may be unbalanced (though perhaps just a physician, which would be fine, yes?). Handwritten or computer-generated, a personal note also reveals a man's command of language; if sent on business letterhead, you get information about his professional affiliation that can be verified. (A quick call to his place of business can confirm whether he's for real.)   Furthermore, requesting an answer by mail may weed out the occasional married man looking for a quick fling (letters take time to write and leave a paper trail).

A fun way to advertise is in a group. That is, you and several like-minded female friends take out an ad together. (This may be the only time I'll encourage you to hang out with other women.) In the ad, you announce that three terrific women will be giving a casual dinner in an undisclosed neighborhood restaurant on such and such a date, and that they seek three terrific men to be their guests. Describe yourselves in general terms, and describe the kinds of men you wish to meet. For example: Three 40-something professional women—fun loving, physically active, and culturally oriented—seek three like-minded men, ages 35 to 55.

This form of advertising has several advantages: It is cheaper to split the cost of an ad rather than foot the bill on your own; inviting three men at a time means you have three chances to meet someone special; since you have to eat dinner anyway, you have not lost much by organizing this evening adventure; and safety in numbers may feel good here. Make sure you pick your female sidekicks wisely, though. If your tastes in men differ radically, you'll have a tough time agreeing on which male respondents to invite.

If you plan to answer some ads, select a flattering photo of yourself and have ten or twenty copies made. (Don't balk at a man's request for a photo, either. Men respond to visuals, remember? Once that checks out for them, they can move on to what really counts. If your particular look doesn't ring his chimes, why would you even want to waste your time going out with him?) If you don't have an attractive, clear photo, ask a relative or friend with proven photographic abilities to photograph you; then select the best pose and make copies.

There are also worthy men who'll only wish to deal by telephone. But if you plan to use the phone for introductions, keep the calls short. The phone should not be used to tell your life story—or to hear his. Use the phone only to establish initial contact, to have a brief, friendly, but not intimate conversation, and to set a mutually convenient time and place to meet in person.

Whether you place or answer ads, or both, certain safety rules apply. Never, ever invite a new man to pick you up at your home or apartment, despite what *I* did in simpler times. (There is no reason for the man even to *know* your address at this point.) Meetings should occur in a public place only—a restaurant, coffee shop, museum, or other establishment. Until you have had a chance to check out the man's background, all subsequent meetings should occur in public, too. This may sound overly cautious, but better to be a wimp than a fool.

Some men's integrity and soundness will be evident to you immediately—for example, you may discover that you have friends in common who can vouch for the man's character, or you may share the same alma mater, in which case you can locate other people who know him. Ask enough specific questions of him to set your mind at ease. He must be affiliated *somewhere*. That is what you want to know. Be smart. If, after several meetings, the things he says do not seem to add up, do not see him again.

How to Read a Personal Ad

Learning to read between the lines of a man's personal ad saves time and annoyance later on. Here are a few tips:

1: If a man feels the need to advertise the number of homes he has or the size of his bank account, his life centers around money, things, and transitory values.

2: A man who says he's "52 but looks 42" probably looks his age and is insecure.

3: A man whose ad tells you he has a great sense of humor, but who has written the ad without an ounce of wit, is probably not all that hilarious after all—but maybe this lack is not a deal-breaker for you.

4: Men fib about their height, just as women fudge about their weight. To get an accurate picture of a new man's true height, deduct two inches from the number he gives you.

5: A man whose ad says he wants "fun," "companionship," "romance," and "a lasting relationship"—or any permutations of the above—does not necessarily seek marriage. If he says he wants fun, companionship, romance, and a lasting relationship "eventually leading to marriage," he can be worked with. However, you need to know what time frame he anticipates. "Eventually" can mean one year or one decade. Then again, it can mean never. (More about this in Chapter Eleven).

Meeting over the Internet

Meeting over the Internet is tricky. While most people use published personal ads to meet and date people in person, practiced surfers of the Internet often use the computer as a way of remaining anonymous and removed.

While some of these folks do hook up with one another after "meeting" through singles "bulletin boards" and in "chat rooms," Internet connections can easily become fantasy substitutes for face-to-face relating. If you are going to use this method of meeting, as with personal ads, make sure you have other means of verifying the person's credibility.

Your Attitude Counts

You now have too many entries for your Time Management Chart—an embarrassment of riches! Remember that this exercise is supposed to be fun. Pace yourself, building more and more new experiences and new people into your life. Do not expect your entire life to change overnight; that is unrealistic. But you will be surprised at how quickly the social landscape can be transformed, and how much better you will begin to feel about the future. But along with an active Time Management Chart must come a personal attitude that complements all your efforts. So here are a few quick tips for making a good impression:

1: First and foremost, as you meet new men, be sure to radiate a sincere love of men in general—not by gushing all over them, of course, but by demonstrating a fundamental appreciation for their strengths. A man can sense whether a woman likes men as a group—or blames all men for the transgressions of a few jerks from her past experience.

2: Smile. No man wants to approach a scowling, sour-faced woman. A smile says you are available for conversation, that you won't bite, that a man can relax in your presence.

3: Thank men when they hold doors open for you or defer to you when exiting an elevator. These good manners deserve to be recognized, and your politeness in turn can lead to more interaction.

4: Make eye contact. All the effective time management in the world comes to naught if a woman habitually looks away self-consciously or refuses to meet a man's gaze. Eye contact tells a man you're open to conversation; staring at the floor merely suggests you'd rather be scrubbing the linoleum.

5: When stuck for a conversation opener, compliment: "What a beautiful tie you're wearing," you offer to the harried but cute executive with whom you're sharing an elevator (it helps if he's wearing one, of course). Men love to be complimented for their attire, their hair, their watches, their hands (and you thought women were the vain ones!). A compliment sets the other person at ease and paves the way for more conversation. Do pick something worthy of being singled out, however, since false admiration usually comes off as such.

6: Take risks. Not stupid ones that jeopardize your personal safety, but emotional risks that expand your horizons.

7: Enjoy yourself. Life can be very sweet. Taste it.

10

The Frog Prince

"Gather around I got
a story to tell
about a Manhattan lady
that I know very well.
She lives at Five Riverside,
her name is Shirley Devore,
and she traveled 'round the world
to meet the guy next door, . . .
You girls who live in apartments,
don't you stare at the wall,
open up the door
and hurry out in the hall . . ."

—John Kander and Fred Ebb, "Ring Them Bells"

These charming lyrics from the Kander and Ebb song reveal the secret we sometimes keep from ourselves: The commoner next door is really a prince.

Five or six years ago, while stopping at a deli for a takeout sandwich, I ran into Sonia, whom I had not seen in a very long time. In her previous incarnation, Sonia had been the very pretty, very glamorous, and very much younger girlfriend of a successful larger-than-life man old enough to be her father. She was still lovely looking, but the 40-ish person who now stood before me wore no makeup and was unadorned, yet she radiated an energy that filled the frame with light. When I commented on her attractive new look, Sonia gushed that she had gone through a lot of changes, had married someone other than her prior steady companion, and was now blissfully happy. Since I was a single woman who longed for a similar fate, I immediately set a lunch date to find out how this woman had achieved her nirvana.

It turned out that Sonia had married her stockbroker, Kenny—a kind, solvent, down-to-earth man her own age whom she had known, and had overlooked as marriage material, for 20 years! While her former gentleman friend had been attentive and generous, he was ambivalent about making a marital commitment to her. She began to see that she had no deep soul connection to this man, whom she knew no better after eight years than she had after eight weeks. They were intimate strangers. It was only when Sonia identified what was missing, and clarified what she actually needed in a mate, that she came to realize that the man with the important qualities she wanted had been in her life all the time.

Since my encounter with Sonia, I have become aware of just how many women have found their matches by reevaluating the men who are already playing a part in their lives. And I see how many more women could experience a similar awakening, if only they were in tune with their needs and recognized the value of the untapped assets in their own portfolios.

Jane Austen understood how readily we overlook the obvious in matters of the heart. When Austen's fictional heroine Emma finally marries Mr. Knightley, her old family friend with whom she's been sparring for years, the wedding commemorates a lifelong affinity. The depth of Emma and Mr. Knightley's abiding connection had never been in doubt; however, Emma had been so busy organizing the love lives of others that she had failed to see that her own ideal mate had been in her company from the start.

Emma has to suffer a certain degree of romantic pain before coming to her senses as regards Mr. Knightley; indeed, her true feelings for him become apparent to her only when she mistakenly believes Mr. Knightley to be engaged to another woman. So inexplicably jealous does Emma become at the thought of this treasured friend's affections being lavished on someone else that she finally gets it: She's in love with him herself!

Discovering romance in the familiar may be less dramatic in real life than in literature, but the results can be equally binding. For me, the love stories of women who find their mates in their own backyards, as it were, are some of the most romantic tales of all. Why? Perhaps because these powerful examples of love transformed demonstrate life's unfailing capacity for mystery and rebirth.

One such example of a romantic awakening concerns Leah, a cousin of my husband's in New York. Attractive and a tireless worker for a nonprofit organization, at age 38 Leah very much wanted to marry. But, while she had dated a fair number of men over the years, none of these relationships had achieved that goal. A brief engagement, when Leah was 33, had ended when she discovered that she and her fiancé had very different expectations of the future they would share. Leah emerged from this aborted trip to the altar a little more cynical and worse for wear.

Gun-shy, she threw herself into her work with redoubled effort. One of her duties was to help enlarge the membership base of her organization. To that end she had targeted a particular independent business owner, Mel, as an ideal candidate. To attract Mel to the organization, Leah arranged several business lunches with him to connect him with like-minded people in her group. Mel became more involved in Leah's organization; they interacted on a regular basis, becoming good friends. Yet, although Mel was divorced, well-heeled, and available, Leah never saw him as even remotely suitable as a mate for her.

Why not? I later asked, once Leah's personal story became known to me. A bit sheepishly, she explained that Mel did not conform to the type of mate she had in mind. When pressed on this point, she said he was less sophisticated than the other men she had dated. In addition, Leah viewed his business life as mundane—he was not a graduate-degreed professional as she was, but rather a self-made businessman. His many achievements, in light of his disadvantaged background, might have struck other women as admirable. For Leah, however, Mel's humble origins were the source of some discomfort. A connection to Mel would not necessarily improve Leah's social status—a factor that apparently carried a lot of weight with her at the time.

Yet she appreciated all the fine qualities Mel possessed—his kindness, patience, generosity, and openness to new ideas. In addition, she saw that Mel truly accepted her for who she was—her elitist and less attractive parts as well as her many wonderful traits. One day, as they lunched at one of their usual haunts and shared horror stories about their recent dates with others, Mel observed that they had never gone out on an official date together. He wondered out loud, Why not?

Over the next three months, Mel gradually wooed Leah away from her preconceived expectations of the type of man she should marry. He had fallen in love with her and wanted her to be his wife. Later, Leah confided that, in her heart, she knew that Mel was good for her and that no one could possibly love her more. She just needed to rewrite the tapes in her head that were getting in the way of her own happiness.

Mel's obvious admiration and respect for Leah—and his willingness to ride out her ambivalence about him without taking it personally—won her over. They eventually married, and she has never looked happier or more relaxed. She and Mel make a complementary couple, benefiting from one of the traditional pluses of the marital bond: They finish off each other, essentially filling in each other's empty spaces. Leah knows she is fortunate to have garnered Mel's level of constancy and devotion, and luckily for her, she recognized her good fortune before it was too late.

Taking Inventory

Leah's story, as well as the story about Sonia that opened this chapter, are instructive for any midlife single in search of a worthy husband. How many women already have good men such as Mel and Kenny in their lives? Not I, you say? We'll see about that.

To find out what may be languishing in your own arsenal, create for yourself an Inventory of Existing Prospects. Using a pad or notebook, make a list of all eligible members of the opposite sex who are currently in your orbit. Candidates can range from best friends and buddies to men you have met only in passing. This includes, but is not limited to, anyone who has shown an interest in you but whose affections you have not returned; anyone you have been involved with in the past for whom you still have warm feelings; anyone from your work or social environment whose romantic potential has not been tested; anyone you come into contact with on a casual or routine basis whose romantic possibilities you may have overlooked or dismissed (your doctor, dentist, lawyer, accountant, stockbroker, pharmacist, restaurateur, and optician; your child's English teacher; your neighbor's son from Cleveland; the trumpet player in Apartment 4G; and so forth). Ultimately, it would be only ethical to discontinue your professional relationship with any doctor, lawyer, or other such professional with whom you became romantically involved. However, merely including such a person's name on the list requires no adjustments.

This list could also include very old loves from your early adulthood—men with whom you shared a powerful attachment but have lost track of, for one reason or another. One rule: These must be men who returned your affections, not men who rebuffed you! In essence, these are relationships in which the feelings were right but the timing was wrong. However, buyer beware: This is not an instruction to break up anyone's marriage. Far from it. A lost love becomes a viable candidate only if he happens to be currently single. If you locate an old flame and find that he is married, you must be prepared to cross off his name from the list.

Your Inventory of Existing Prospects should not include anyone who has treated you badly over time or anyone who is otherwise of questionable character. Nor should it include anyone whom you know going in has a value system radically different from your own.

After each entry on your list, fill in your reasons for believing this person could not be a good mate for you. Then, for each reason that has caused a man to be written off, ask yourself, on what have I based this judgment? The key to this exercise lies in the previous sentence. While people often know the reasons they have discounted a particular candidate, those reasons are often bogus or have been hastily formulated. The assignment forces you to examine your beliefs and to write off no one without just cause. More often than not, there will be a viable prospect on the page.

If next to "Roger's" name you have written "obnoxious," "abusive," "emotionally damaged," or some other harsh observation, chances are good that you will never view Roger in a more favorable light. And probably with good reason. Such traits do not feel negotiable. If, however, your reasons for excluding Roger seem more subjective, then Roger deserves a second look. Subjective reasons for giving Roger the thumbs down might be such descriptions as "goofy but nice," "too young," "intentions unclear," or "not a lot of chemistry."

If Roger strikes you as being a lovely fellow but tends to clown around in social situations, *this* can be worked with. He does not have a character disorder, merely an annoying behavior. Perhaps if you better understood his need to play the court jester, you would be less hard on him for it. And if you got to know him better, perhaps the fact that you like him best when he's not "performing" would lessen his need to seek such negative attention.

Women often rule out men who are only five (or even fewer) years their junior, thinking that the man shouldn't be younger than they, period. If in fact the age factor has been Roger's death knell, you might ask yourself, "Too young for what?" A 48-year-old woman marrying a 15-year-old boy would be against the law. But if Roger clocks in at only eight or ten years younger than you, do not hold this against him. Remember, men have been marrying women younger than they since the beginning of time! And, of course, your pool of eligible men expands exponentially once you open your mind to age brackets below your own. What really matters more is whether the man finds the age difference a problem. If he does not, consider all the positives that a match with a younger man affords! A more active sex life? Fewer years as a widow? You get what I mean.

"Intentions unclear," a response one of my clients gave about a man on her prospects list, is a poor reason to delete a candidate. Murky intentions can be made less murky. If a man you like has been giving you mixed signals about his romantic leanings, let him know—nicely, of course—that you need some clarification. Without attacking him, or making him feel defensive or embarrassed, ask him to help you understand what's going on. Assure him that you do find him attractive, but that games bore you. In response, he will either declare himself (hooray!) or act as though you've been smoking something illegal. In the latter instance, he actually may be surprised that you read something into his behavior, or he simply may be playing mind games with you. Whatever the truth, your problem has been solved: This man does not qualify as an existing prospect; now you can eliminate him in good conscience. See how easy that was?

"Not a lot of chemistry" is a common reason why women cross men off their lists. Yet chemistry is, at best, elusive. If it were a fixed quality between individuals, all those people who experience "love at first sight" would remain "in love" forever. And we know from staggering divorce statistics that this is not the reality. So be suspicious of your own conclusions when axing a good man for lack of chemistry. Good chemistry *can* evolve (though not in every case, of course), while waning passion almost always moves further into the abyss. (More on chemistry later in this chapter.)

One client of mine in particular, Alison, benefited greatly from reassessing the men on her Inventory of Existing Prospects. Alison had placed George's name on her list, along with the names of four or five other men. She had met George (who, like herself, was in his 40s) through a hiking club to which they both belonged—a group that met every weekend to conquer a piece of nearby terrain.

Alison and George had a lot in common, and, more often than not, they ended up on the trail together, chattering about a range of mutual interests as they puffed their way up the slope. One Sunday, after their customary hike, George suggested they grab some lunch at a nearby restaurant, an invitation Alison accepted eagerly. But she was crestfallen when the bill came, and it appeared the check would be split. With a sinking feeling, Alison laid down her American Express card next to his.

When Alison entered George's name on her Inventory of Existing Prospects, she wrote next to it the word "cheap." This trait, which she could not abide in a suitor, had been George's undoing. I questioned Alison about George, and it became apparent that, apart from this one negative, she viewed him as a great guy. Bright, attractive, and happily engaged in his chosen profession, he struck Alison as being solid and admirable, interested in other people, the kind of man you could lean on in a crisis and whose company would never bore her. And, yes, she felt they had good chemistry.

Perhaps she had judged George too hastily, I offered. Maybe there was an explanation for his seemingly ungallant behavior—an explanation that went beyond information she had at her disposal. Alison agreed to reserve judgment a bit longer and accepted George's subsequent invitations to spend more time together away from the hiking trail. In fact, she reciprocated with invitations of her own.

Eventually, their relationship evolved into a romance, and she learned something interesting about that unsettling "first date": In George's mind, the Dutch treat lunch had not been a date at all—merely a case of two friends going out for a bite. But as George later explained to Alison, he began to fall in love with her. And once that happened, he no longer viewed her as a buddy only; in his eyes, she had become a woman to protect and nurture as well. George, a product of his masculine culture, then felt it natural to pick up the check.

Whether or not one believes that men in dating situations should be responsible for paying the tab obscures the point. The issue here is that Alison had made a judgment about a man—and had proceeded to write him off—based on insufficient data. Had she not reassessed her position and given George a second look, they never would have gotten married—an event that took place recently, to the delight of many friends, including this author!

Chemistry 101

The story of Isaac and Rebekah—the Old Testament matriarch whose willingness to venture far from her family's home changed the course of biblical history—reveals a great deal about the nature of marital love. Consider the structure of this passage from the Book of Genesis: Isaac "married Rebekah, and she became his wife ... and he loved her." He married her first, the passage tells us, and then he loved her as a consequence of having done so. Their commitment to each other, and their deep bond, came first. This was the foundation upon which Isaac and Rebekah built their home together; the love that filled that home was a skill they learned later on.

Why is this ancient story, perhaps no more than an allegory, relevant to modern women at the twilight of the twentieth century? After all, have we not been trained that sexual entitlement is one of our sacred rights, along with equal pay for equal work and the vote? Are we not justified in expecting that we should have passionate feelings for any man we would place on a list of existing marital prospects? Yes and no. What this limited thinking fails to address is that passion between two people who like, respect, and enjoy each other can grow over time.

Clinical psychologist Judith Wallerstein, in her absorbing book *The Good Marriage*, shares the results of her extensive study of long-married couples. All the couples in Wallerstein's sample had been married to each other a minimum of ten years, and all had characterized their relationships as happy ones. Not surprisingly, these couples offer great insight into the role sex plays in enduring marital contentment.

Drawing from her research, the author isolates four marriage models—what she calls the "romantic," the "rescue," the "companionate," and the "traditional" models. While the vast majority of couples in Wallerstein's study affirmed the importance of satisfying sex in their long-term happiness, only the couples involved in the "romantic" model—15 percent of the entire sample—said that sexual chemistry was at the top of their list of priorities. Put another way, 85 percent of these spouses cited other elements as more germane to the health of their marriages— children, trust, friendship, shared values, humor, and understanding were the most frequently mentioned contributors. In addition, of the 85 percent for whom these other factors carried great weight, a sizable portion felt that the depth of their connection on these other levels in fact had enhanced their shared sexual lives. "Some spoke of the passionate love that began their relationship," Wallerstein elaborates, "but for a surprising number, love grew in the rich soil of the marriage, nourished by emotional and physical intimacy, appreciation, and fond memories."

Wallerstein's findings remind me of a truism once quoted to me by a friend: "Lust is what you feel right now; love is what you will feel later if everything else is right." Since chemistry between loving, dynamic partners can actually intensify over time, I always advise my clients to reconsider even those existing prospects with whom they seemingly have no palpable chemistry. The distinction that does matter is between feeling completely turned off by a man vs. being merely neutral. If you are truly repelled by a prospect, it's fair to consider that a clear signal not to pursue things. Within the neutral zone, however, there is potential for erotic feelings to grow. Midlife singles who wish to marry need to explore this uncharted territory with the good men already in their midst. When a woman says to me, "But I don't think of him in *that* way," I always recommend, "Think again."

Some women worry that testing the chemical component to a friendship or acquaintanceship will ruin it should either party wish to discontinue the romance. However, among mature, communicative adults, this need not happen. A strong bond of friendship should be able to withstand a momentary glitch, should there be one, without destroying all the good things that came before. In my opinion, the greater concern a woman should have is this: By failing to test the romantic potential of a good man, she loses the opportunity for marriage to someone who already knows, cares for, and appreciates her. Where else will she find such favorable odds right out of the starting gate?

The value of remaining open to this more gradual path to romance and marriage crystallized for me in the experience of my brother's friend Jill. A dynamo in her late 30s who now lives in Dallas, Jill recently married one of her best friends, Andrew, her colleague and buddy for ten years. Jill often commented that her relationship with Andrew mirrored her rapport with intimate female friends—they could talk about everything (and did), and when they took vacations together, sometimes they even shared a room (she wore flannel jammies, no doubt). Jill complained to Andrew about her boyfriend troubles, her current crises at work, even her cramps. He knew her worst side as well as her best, including what she looked like with a green, 30-minute face mask plastered to her skin. In turn, Jill listened to Andrew's worries and concerns and offered advice and support on matters personal and professional.

Since Jill worked in a trendy, male-dominated business, she was accustomed to harmless platonic flirting with the single men around her. Andrew had been a recipient of Jill's playfulness, but in ten years, they never so much as kissed each other.

Then several events occurred that threw reality into bold relief for Jill. First, her current steady boyfriend died in a tragic sporting accident. Their relationship recently had become serious, and Jill had believed they would soon announce their engagement. Grieving and depressed, she leaned on Andrew for the moral support he had always provided and found comfort in his reassuring friendship. Some months later, on a Saturday night when neither of them had a date and ended up with each other, a second punch came her way: In response to Jill's global prognostication that she would never love again, her dear friend Andrew whispered, "I've been in love with you for ten years, what about me?"

Jill's eyes filled with tears, and in that moment she felt in her gut that this was as right as rain. Jill now believes that, had she not lost her then boyfriend—which put life's fragility so much in perspective for her—she never would have recognized the depth of what Andrew had to offer. She married Andrew—a man who treats her with enormous love and tenderness and whose devotion has only increased since their wedding day. "I married him because I respect him so," she later explained, "and because he will make a wonderful father to our unborn children. He knows me, and he loves me anyway." She laughs good-naturedly. "I could never do better than Andrew." And everyone who knows them agrees.

Where Do I Go from Here?

If you have been using your Time Management Chart and your Master List to their fullest capacity, and if you have conducted a thorough Inventory of Existing Prospects (each of these is an ongoing process) you may have targeted a man who shows promise as a marriage candidate. (If not, continue incorporating these principles into your daily life, and—as the saying goes—"he will come.") In any event, you may now wonder what to do with such a man once you find him. The following chapter leaves nothing in doubt on this crucial topic.

11

Interview Your Prospect

Women request estimates from contractors before remodeling their houses. And they wouldn't hire a new employee without a reference check. Yet they easily fall into bed with a new man without knowing a thing about his character, his track record, or his intentions.

Unwilling to make such a blind investment myself, I "interviewed" my now-husband before beginning a romance with him—a notion that many women find amusing, foreign, or just plain incomprehensible. But in actuality, screening your man is a rational way to maximize your chances for marriage.

Reflect on important relationships that you have had

that did not end in marriage, either because the man in question turned out to be someone other than he "seemed," or because the man would not commit to you, or both. Count the months or years you may have spent in dead-end relationships. String the years end to end and visualize how much of your life has been taken up by men who could not deliver what you needed. How much time and emotional energy would you have conserved had these men been properly screened in the early stages of dating, before anyone even removed a sock? Now, face the current reality: If you wish to marry after 35, you can no longer afford to waste more time with unmarriageable men. Period.

As I have shared throughout this book, my numerous false steps and detours to the altar taught me some valuable lessons:

- To proactively seek out environments in which I would come into contact with eligible men.

- To stay focused and clear about what I needed.

- To listen, no matter how disheartening the truth.

- To walk away from Nowhere Men the minute I spotted them.

- To look beyond the gloss of a man to the person within.

In sum, my past taught me how to be a good interviewer, so that by the time I met my now-husband, I had the proper tools for separating a gemstone from the faux.

To be a good interviewer does not mean you assault a man with a barrage of impertinent questions. Nor does it require that you dress up in a police uniform and conduct a psychological interrogation of the suspect under a highbeam lamp. (You may *wish* to do these things, but such tactics would be counterproductive, right?) No, a good interviewer like you understands subtlety and nuance. You are an information gatherer, a keen observer who collects data to see if a story holds up. In addition to asking key questions, you are a consummate listener at this point (remember Chapter Four?), who refines her knowledge of a new man by spending time with him in a variety of situations and circumstances. Taken seriously, the interview process can wipe the phrase "unlucky in love" from your vocabulary.

The questions and issues that form the interview process can be broken down into three levels, or stages. Stage I involves learning about a man's *character*. It focuses on finding out about the man himself, separate and apart from his feelings for you. (His feelings for you become relevant only after you've ascertained your own degree of interest in him.) Stage I is a crucial step in adequately assessing your man's worth and his marriageability.

Stage II questions follow naturally from your fact-finding mission in Stage I, and concern your new man *in relation to you, specifically*. If you've arrived at Stage II, the assumption is that your man has come through Stage I with some degree of success. (If you find yourself posing a lot of Stage II questions without already feeling good about Stage I, go back to the Stage I issues and make sure this man is a suitable prospect before proceeding.)

Stage III relates to the *type of life the two of you envision together*. Arriving at Stage III presupposes that your man has come through Stages I and II with flying colors and that the two of you have discussed the possibility of marriage. It should not take years to arrive at Stage III, but there are no guaranteed shortcuts, either. If you've gotten to Stage III without delving into the issues represented by Stages I and

II, chances are you're operating more on fantasy than fact. Make the interview process work *for* you by respecting it and using it correctly.

Stage 1

Let us assume you have just met a new man, "Peter," while you were taking tennis lessons at the public courts in your city. You're intrigued by Peter, and he appears to be equally taken with you. The two of you begin to date. What information can you learn about Peter in Stage I? By observing his behavior and asking yourself certain key questions, you'll be able to form impressions about his value system. These pictures can be rounded out by asking Peter occasional benign questions that reveal deeper truths about his priorities, his beliefs, and his essential nature. Among the areas to consider:

Values

What values does he emphasize in the choices he makes? Does he operate from a perspective of materialism? Career? Spirituality? Family cohesiveness? Pure self-interest? Community and civic concerns? Or a blend of these? Are the values he affirms by the way he lives compatible with the values that govern your own life?

The implication here is not that you must be clones of each other, but that your values should not be directly at odds, either. A male friend, a successful corporate attorney, recently split up with his lovely 40-year-old girlfriend because she had no respect for the nature of his work. Her deeply ingrained antibusiness bias caused a lot of conflict in their relationship. Since she disapproved of the part of him that gave him the greatest satisfaction, they were obviously mismatched, and had been mismatched since day one. "She was never going to admire me," he explained, "no matter how many cases I won. I didn't want to live with such disapproval." One can hardly fault my friend for his feelings. But wouldn't his marriage-minded girlfriend have been better off to examine the incompatibilities in their relationship earlier, before spending three years with a man whose values so clashed with her own?

Respect

A second question for you to ponder vis-à-vis a new man concerns his behavior toward others. How does he treat people in less powerful positions than his own—waiters, clerks, his employees, and so forth? Is he respectful and fair? Or is he a man who must dominate those around him to feel big?

Family

If he has children from a prior marriage, does he have a good relationship with them? Has he been an active father, or did he allow himself to become the proverbial absentee dad? If he's estranged from any of his children, has he made efforts to repair the situation? Or does he just throw up his hands in defeat?

Women sometimes assume that a man who exhibits only limited commitment to a first family will be a better catch than a committed one, since this theoretically means he'll have more time for a new family. In actuality, a man who so blithely turns his back on his primary dependents may not have a lot to offer a second family, either. A woman who finds this sort of careless behavior desirable may be in for a rude awakening.

It is also telling whether he has been circumspect about

introducing you to his children or whether he has been in an enormous rush to ram you into the family constellation. A man who wants to get to know you first, before opening the relationship to his family at-large, is exercising good judgment, while a man who is too much in a hurry may be more interested in the *idea* of you and the role you might play in his family life than in you. Conversely, down the line, a man who keeps you a secret from his children after six or seven months of dating does not intend to marry you. Exceptions exist, of course, but at a certain point, a man who is serious about you should want to show you off and incorporate you into his personal world.

It is tried and true wisdom that you can tell a lot about a man by how he treats and describes his mother. I am always astonished when women neglect to note any connection between a man's behavior toward his own mother and his eventual treatment of them. If he is on good terms with his mother and has forged a workable rapport with her, he probably has a fairly positive model for male/female interactions. On the other hand, if he shows Mom little respect, is dismissive of her, has poor communication with her, or regards her with great mistrust, you'll probably have trouble achieving parity in this relationship. This does not mean that the relationship can't work, merely that you'll experience the fallout from this man's unresolved issues with Mom.

Consideration

Is he on time for your dates and appointments? Or is he habitually late? Occasional tardiness is human—and unavoidable—while chronic lateness indicates the other person perceives his time to be more valuable than yours. It also indicates a general lack of regard for you. Similarly telling is whether he honors his commitments by making good on promises to family, friends, and colleagues. Does he let things slide without acknowledging his obligation to behave responsibly? If he has this bad habit, recognize that commitments made to you or your relationship may be similarly flimsy.

Solvency

Is his financial house in order? Does he have reliable, legal sources of income? How many people does he support? The financial truth about a man can be slippery to grasp, since appearances and reality can be at odds. But a man's attitude about money is usually apparent. If he's cautious and conservative in his expenditures, he's probably not the type to be $100,000 in hock to a bookie. But you *never* know for sure! Keep your eyes and ears open, and don't be fooled by fancy trappings such as expensive cars, boats, and the like, which can be repossessed overnight. A related question is whether he has a solid, defensible work history. Does his résumé reflect a hodgepodge of comings and goings? As in tennis, consistency counts here.

References

Does he have good friends to whom you have been introduced and whose appeal as friends makes sense to you? What do they say about him? About his previous romantic attachments? Or does he seem to have arrived out of nowhere, with no friends or backstory to share? A man with a mysterious past is sexy only in the movies; in real life, he is bad news.

Balance

How does he prioritize his time with respect to work and personal life obligations? Does he strive for a balance—as difficult as that may be to achieve? Or does work always seem to come first? Remember, the attitude he displays toward his work now is the one you'll be living with later, if you end up with this man. In general, is he moderate in his relationships with alcohol, food, and other substances? Or do you observe poor impulse control here? If this man has loose boundaries in this arena, you may wish to rethink an intimate involvement with him.

Stage II

Stage II questions can come up at almost any time in the early phase of a relationship, and they sometimes do overlap Stage I issues. However, Stage II questions matter most once you have decided how interested you are in a given prospect.

Access

Does he ask you out for weekend dates in addition to weeknight invitations? Or has he relegated you to a once-per-week, Thursday-night slot? A man who is genuinely interested in you should want to see you more than once a week, and he should definitely want to see you on weekends. Women often wonder whether a man who keeps their dates conveniently restricted to one day during the week can possibly be all that interested, and, regrettably, my answer to them is no. If you are not his weekend choice, you should assume that someone else is.

Concern

Is he genuinely interested in you—your hopes, dreams, accomplishments, setbacks? Or is he much more wrapped up in himself? A man whose attraction to you is ongoing and growing should want to know more and more about you. If his main focus continues to be himself, he's either very self-centered or just not that taken with you—or very possibly both.

Does pleasing you matter to him? Does he solicit, and honor, your feelings about which movies to see, which restaurants to eat in, and what activities you'll do together? A man who likes you should want to make you happy. If he ignores your preferences, he probably isn't your man— unless a 90/10 relationship turns you on.

Your Kids

If you have children still under your roof, does he accept them as part of the package that is you? Or does he seem resentful or jealous of the time you give to them? A man who is going to be an appropriate match for you will be one who understands your responsibilities and priorities as a good mother.

Sharing

Do you find the lines of communication between the two of you open and clear? Are you comfortable discussing personal topics with each other? Does he make it easy for you to share confidences? Or does he inhibit this sort of talk by being judgmental, narrow-minded, impatient, or closed-off?

Chemistry

Is there a comfortable physical attraction between the two of you? Or does the chemistry between you feel forced right now? Remember that erotic feelings can grow between two people who are well matched in other ways, so give yourself time before judging whether you and he can be physically compatible.

Socializing

Do you enjoy being together in public, finding a relaxed style as a couple? Or does being out among others put a strain on your relationship? Apart from the adjustment of blending into each other's social lives, being around other people should be a relative pleasure, not a stresser.

Trust

Do you inspire confidence in each other at public gatherings? Or does the presence of other people incite jealousy? When you're apart, do you feel secure about his whereabouts, or do you worry about what he might be doing in your absence? Again, a good relationship between mature people should not provoke insecurities in either partner.

Fondness

When you're apart, do you think about him and look forward to seeing him again? Do you want to share with him later on the experiences you have when the two of you are apart?

Comfort

Can you be playful, silly, or even a little weird in his presence and know he will understand? Or do you feel constrained to behave always in a predictably mature and ladylike way? If people are well matched, both parties should feel free to express occasional eccentricities or inconsistencies without fear of condemnation.

The specific issues you address at this point in your relationship will vary somewhat depending on the profile of the man involved. So, in addition to the questions I have enumerated, think of others that apply to your particular situation. If you cannot think of any questions to ask yourself in this regard, perhaps you are uncomfortable knowing the full story about your man. A reluctance to examine the health of your relationship, though, does not bode well for its long-range survival. In the final analysis, a relationship that is going to work should hold up under close scrutiny. This does not mean that every problem or dilemma will have been ironed out prior to marriage. But it does mean that the core issues affecting you as a couple will have been acknowledged.

The Golden Rule

To interview the man in your life using the Stage I and II questions outlined above presupposes that you have postponed sleeping with him. If you just stumbled on that last sentence, it bears repeating: If you are going about the interview process correctly, you should not become sexually intimate with your special man until Stage II has been completed with positive and reassuring results. This rule is non-negotiable.

Such an edict is not intended as a punishment, nor is it a ploy for manipulating a man into a commitment. Delaying sex has real, observable benefits for the *woman*. But these benefits do not accrue to the vast majority of women, because they ignore this valuable message, erroneously believing that sex will make a man feel more attached to them. In truth, it is the woman who more often feels bound and committed once sex has become part of the equation.

A woman who is dating to find a husband, as opposed to dating to pass the time, has no business sleeping with a man for whom the possibility of marriage is a problem. There are no exceptions to this rule. And the way to enforce it is to delay having sex until you know your man is a worthy and marriageable person in whom to invest your time and emotional energy. A man who truly cares for a woman will go along with her desire to move slowly; a man who gives her a lot of static about it probably does not qualify as a long-distance runner and should be cut loose.

A woman who postpones sex until her man's willingness to marry is clear protects herself from attaching to an unworthy candidate or to one who does not intend to marry. It is easier to see a man's true character while he still has his clothes on; and if he turns out not to be as fine as he "seemed," or to be unmarriageable, it is emotionally easier for a woman to walk away from him if she has not yet shared herself sexually.

Look at the downside: A woman leaps into bed quickly and finds herself hooked. Once hooked, she must then justify her choice of the man—even if he soon turns out to be undeserving of her esteem. If unfavorable truths about him begin to crop up, the woman who has made a careless sexual investment tends to look the other way, or she rationalizes to herself that what she's seeing isn't all that negative. She sugarcoats reality to avoid being alone, or to avoid admitting she's made a potentially embarrassing mistake.

Time and again, I watch women backpedaling in this way. Months, sometimes years, are wasted in the service of preserving a fiction. Had the relationship remained presexual longer, the woman would have seen the red flags sooner; she then could have moved on swiftly to a more appropriate prospect.

Women often ask me to specify how many weeks or months should have elapsed before sex becomes part of the relationship. There is no one right answer to this question.

What is essential is that the issues suggested by the Stage I and Stage II questions have been addressed to your satisfaction, that the man's long-term commitment to you is clear, and that you genuinely return his feelings. This level of understanding is rarely achieved in a matter of weeks; it generally requires months and months of getting to know a man before all the necessary information has come forward. By delaying sex in this fashion, you allow the interview process to work for you, and you confirm your own ability to interest a man beyond the confines of the bedroom.

Separating the Wheat from the Chaff

How does one know if a man is marriageable? The way to separate the buyers from the browsers—the only reliable way—is to go on record as being a buyer yourself. The browsers will stealthily slink out of the store at this point, and that is the whole idea. The men who are not serious will now be free to waste the time of less diligent, or less marriage-minded, women; while the men who are still in the store will be ripe candidates for the role of spouse.

At what point do you declare yourself a buyer and find out whether the man in question is also a serious shopper? The best time is while you're exploring the Stage I questions listed earlier. But how, specifically, does one broach this delicate topic with a man? To give you some ideas, I have written a brief scenario drawn from the experiences of real women who successfully discussed the issue of marriage early in their relationships with men—men whom they later married! The narrator of the script, "Barbara," is a composite of these women; if you use the script as your guide, it can work for you, too. Here is what Barbara has to say:

We had been seeing each other approximately three times a week for about six weeks. In advance of one of our dates, I told Dan by phone that I had something important to discuss with him that evening. After dinner at an Italian restaurant, we came back to my place; I offered him a snifter of good brandy, and he went to sit in the living room, apparently all ears.

I began by telling him how much fun I had been having since meeting him, reinforcing all the positive thoughts I had about the time we had been spending together. He agreed that, yes, it had all been very nice. And I would love for things to continue this way, I ventured, so that I can get to know you even better. He nodded in agreement, delighted that the conversation was taking such a pleasant turn. But there is one matter I do need to clarify, I offered, as he picked up a hint of hesitation.

From here I launched into my spiel: I was 41 and was finally ready to settle down. I was dating for a purpose, I confided—to find a mate, not to pass the time or merely to have fun. He was a 43-year-old bachelor who had never been married, I observed. (With this, Dan shifted visibly in his seat.) Perhaps marriage was not a goal of his, I offered understandingly. And this was his prerogative, of course. But since I *was* dating for a purpose, I could only continue dating a given man—and begin an intimate involvement with him—if he were dating for the same reason I was. I have absolutely no idea whether you're the man for me, I added, letting him off the hook. (And at that point, I *didn't* know.) Maybe you are, and maybe you aren't. Only time would tell me that. But I don't have the luxury of finding out unless I know that your ultimate goals are compatible with mine. After all, I reasoned, it would be quite a waste of our mutual time if we continued to date knowing that our goals were so divergent.

It was all very logical, spread out before us like a road map for which I was discussing the most direct route to a destination. I wasn't telling him I was in love with him, or that I wanted to marry *him* specifically. No threats, no ultimatums. Just a soft-spoken articulation of the facts as I saw them. I eagerly awaited his response.

Dan was visibly touched by the words I had spoken. He was dating for the same reason I was, he assured me. He felt he had been single long enough; he was ready for the next phase of his life. He had been feeling this way for some time, he continued, had even been engaged briefly several years ago and would have married the woman, had she not turned out to be less solid than she originally seemed. He then told me that he appreciated my having raised this whole issue. Indeed, he did appear more relaxed now that my "important" topic had been aired.

Once he agreed that, in principle, marriage was his goal, too, I told him more about what I needed in a mate: In addition to marriage, I also saw motherhood in my future; any man with whom I began a romance would also need to be open to the idea of children. A man for whom this idea might be a problem would be an inappropriate companion for me. Dan quickly indicated that being a parent was something he wanted, as well. He assumed that family, as well as marriage, would be part of his future.

I exhaled. He genuinely wanted the same things I wanted. The next step? I suggested that, at our ages, it should not take years to figure out whether we might be "right" for each other. And he agreed that, yes, it should not take years. It should take only a matter of months, I continued. And he said that sounded right. Seven or eight, don't you think? I queried, again looking for consensus. Eight sounded about right, he said, picking the longer time frame. That would put us at about May, I responded, establishing a deadline without calling it that. So by May of next year we should be able to decide whether this is a match.

The line in the sand had been drawn. We would give ourselves an eight-month romance, during which time we would evaluate whether to make it a lifelong commitment. If yes, we would become engaged. If no, we would each move on.

The timetable that Barbara set up with Dan for determining their marital suitability may strike you as being rushed. But think how leisurely it is when compared to the speed with which most dating couples become sexually intimate!

In truth, mature people who have clarified their goals, have interviewed each other and listened carefully to what has been said, and have delayed lovemaking until the initial screening represented by Stages I and II has been done, do not need years to "figure things out." Unlike 22-year-olds, whose identities are still shifting, mature people come to the dating arena with their philosophies, priorities, and lifestyles fairly established. For them, the issue of choosing a mate becomes one of compatibility within relatively fixed boundaries.

Notice that at each juncture in Barbara's conversation with Dan she elicited agreement on the point at hand: (1) that he was dating for marriage; (2) that becoming a father was a positive concept for him; (3) that a finite amount of time should be allotted to their dating relationship; and (4) that eight months would be the appropriate amount of time during which to reach a decision about a future together.

Achieving a man's agreement at each step of the conversation is crucial. Once he has indicated consensus on a particular issue, he has become a partner in the process. He therefore need not feel backed into a corner or railroaded into a relationship he does not want. If a man cannot give his agreement to the core issues as you raise them, he probably is not a marriageable man—at least, not to you. And if he can agree on the core issues, then setting a finite time frame for exploring your relationship prevents each of you from taking the other for granted. It helps each of you stay focused on the purpose of your romantic involvement.

A man who has agreed to a finite time frame in which the two of you will decide whether to marry may ask for an "extension" of time once the cutoff date has been reached. If, by the cutoff date, you've already decided you want to marry the guy, do not panic; cheerfully agree to a short extension—three months at the most. But it is imperative that you clarify the purpose of the extra time. What does he want to know that he has not already found out? What new information does he need to make a final decision? Often, the request for more time simply reflects a man's general anxiety about taking the big plunge. But sometimes specific relationship issues need to be ironed out before he can be certain of his decision. In any case, once the additional time has elapsed, he must commit, or you must move on. But rest assured that almost all men who have gone this far with you in the process will make a marital commitment. Remember, you weeded out the casual browsers and game players a long time ago!

All well and good, you lament. But what about old-fashioned feminine mystery? How can a woman hope to acquire a husband by being so up front? Doesn't a man need to feel the challenge of the chase in order to succumb? Popular rules to the contrary, the classic male/female dance can too easily box a woman into a corner if it's the only step she knows.

While you're clarifying that a particular man is marriageable, there is plenty of room for flirtation, playfulness, and even a little competition for your attentions. But to play a calculating game of now you see me, now you don't with a man who has no intention of marrying is a woeful waste of time. It is doubtful that any amount of feminine mystery, clever manipulation, or measured disinterest is going to alter the ultimate outcome with such a man. You may be able to string him along for a while, even watch him jump through hoops as you spin your magic web. But at the end of the road, you probably will be exhausted by this man, not married to him.

In the less likely event that you actually manipulate such a man into a marriage with you, the only way you will have your needs met by him in the future is through more deception. Is this the way you want to spend the rest of your life? How secure will you be in his love if it is built on a lie? What are the odds that such a marriage can last? In general, men who are marriageable are marriageable without a lot of tricks, while unmarriageable men remain that way no matter how sophisticated the snare. A woman who thinks she bagged her man because of her clever manipulations overestimates herself and underestimates her man. In all likelihood, he was *ready* to be caught by the right woman.

Further Mistakes to Avoid

No matter how careful a woman is in making her lists of priorities and eligible men, the preparation goes to waste if the
woman is her own worst enemy. Right from the first introduction, or the first date, some women tip the scales in a
way that puts them at a distinct disadvantage. In what ways
do women subvert their ability to make the interview
process work for them?

Withholding Key Desires

At the movies not long ago, I overheard a disturbing
conversation between a mother and daughter seated next to
me. The daughter was relating a story about her 30-some-
thing girlfriend who had recently become engaged to a man
in his 50s. It seems the man had made it clear from the
beginning that he did not want more children (he already
had two grown children from a previous marriage). Given
this fact, the young woman, who fervently wanted a baby,
had decided to hide her true feelings from him until after
their wedding. She would "change his mind" later, she had
confided to her girlfriend, as though the task would be as
simple as altering a dress. The sadness here is that neither
the bride-to-be nor her unsuspecting partner will come out
of this manipulation fulfilled. Even if she does change her
husband's mind, or trick him into a pregnancy, her baby will
be stuck with a resentful father. Everyone suffers when basic
needs are not articulated up front.

Spilling the Beans

A common error is the long, rambling phone call—
those late-night talkathons in which a woman reveals to a
man she barely knows all the gory details of her life. Such
oral excess may make her feel closer to the man, but it does

236 How to Get Married After 35

nothing to magnetize her to him. Revelations are for the therapist's couch or the church confessional, not the early stage of dating. Keep phone calls brief, pleasurable, and alluring. A man should hang up wishing you could stay on the line longer. If he knows everything about you from day one, there is nothing left to discover. This is one of those instances in which less is definitely more.

Too Much Too Soon

Giving too much too soon is a classic female faux pas in the initial phase of knowing a man. This includes not only the premature sharing of sex, as just discussed, but also the hundred and one overeager gestures women make in hopes of pleasing a given prospect and binding him to her. I know a woman who flew halfway around the world—at her own expense!—to spend four days with a man with whom she had had only three dates. Now *that's* excessive. Her lack of restraint threw the interaction off center. The man quickly began to take her for granted, while simultaneously she began making unreasonable demands on him—payback for her too-generous overture. What might have developed into a mutually satisfying relationship blew up in smoke.

A more mundane example of giving too much too soon is the woman who sent chicken soup to a colleague of mine with whom she'd had one date the night before—a date cut short by the man's incipient flu. The soup arrived warm, along with a handwritten note telling him to "Feel better *bubbele*" (Yiddish for "sweetie"). This chicken soup gambit was cloying and unsexy. No matter what the circumstances, offering a gift after one date is smothering; and offering such a maternal gift is hardly a romantic choice—not unless one knows that the man in question responds positively to such cues (for this particular man, it was the kiss of death!).

Compromising on the Essentials and Bending Over Backwards

Too many compromises up front? If this characterizes your behavior in the early stages of a relationship, curb it! Whether she's ignoring the fact that the man doesn't want to marry, or suppressing her own likes and dislikes to catch him, a woman who must turn herself inside out to be with a particular man has attached to the wrong guy. While the give-and-take in a relationship rarely breaks down to a 50/50 split, a substantial imbalance in this department indicates trouble.

Taking Early Retirement

Do you remove yourself from the dating circuit as soon as you meet a new man you like? When a woman cuts herself off in such a fashion, she virtually disregards all other marital prospects before she has a clue about her new man's marriageability. And, of course, if she has prematurely begun a sexual relationship with the new man before she has gauged his intentions, she has propelled herself even further into an undesirable corner.

Remember those great romantic stories our mothers told us about the multiple suitors who populated their personal lives? Men who actually competed with one another for a woman's affections? Such social conventions existed because more women of our mothers' generation played the field; they had multiple suitors—and, therefore, choices!—because they commonly dated more than one man at a time, delaying sex until a man had declared his love and proposed, or in many cases, actually married them. There is wisdom here that eludes women who think themselves modern just because they can undress on the second or third date.

He's Not Retired and You Didn't Know It

Finally, women place themselves at a disadvantage with men by assuming that a given relationship is an exclusive monogamous one without having a discussion about it; or by assuming that the man's intentions are toward marriage without ever ascertaining his marriageability. In no other arena of one's life would such fantasy assumptions rule. You would not bid on a pretty house without obtaining a thorough inspection of its foundation, its wiring, plumbing, and general health. Why then would you wager your own happiness on such meager and incomplete information?

Stage III

We shall assume now that the ideas in this book have had some impact on your thinking and that whatever mistakes you once made in the early stages of relationships are well behind you.

Now we return to Peter, whom you have been dating for four or five months. Before your relationship took a sexual turn, you asked all the right questions, observed Peter's character in action, and determined that, indeed, he was a marriageable man. He may well be your future husband. What questions need to be addressed by two people like you who now contemplate marriage?

The more willing you are to explore these issues, the more smoothly you will ease into married life. Blending two worlds into one need not cause too much stress—some, of course, but not too much!—if the parties share their assumptions. Problems arise when individual expectations remain in one's head rather than being laid on the table.

All couples should discuss certain key issues before

deciding to tie the knot, and the sooner you're comfortable raising them with each other, the less time you'll waste with an ultimately incompatible match.

Money

Financial matters, often the most uncomfortable to grapple with up front, can be the source of the greatest conflict in an intimate relationship. To promote harmony down the line, discuss how you plan to handle joint finances. Will both of you continue to work? How will your individual salaries and other assets be treated? Which one of you will actually pay the bills? What percentage of your joint income will be allotted to savings? What portion of either income will be allocated to existing children or ex-spouses? How do you anticipate providing for each other in your wills? Do you expect to sign a prenuptial agreement?

Some women assume that these issues will "work themselves out" as the marriage goes along. And inevitably, these matters do get resolved. But to leave such important questions purely to chance weakens your ability to negotiate with each other effectively and can be the source of tremendous disharmony in your marriage.

A friend of mine married a divorced man who had three children, seven, eight, and ten years of age, for whom he was the custodial parent. She and this man had dated for three years before marrying, during which time my friend invested a lot of energy nurturing his kids. Several years into the marriage, my friend learned that the lovely house in which they resided was still listed in the children's names only, with no reference to joint ownership with her. This meant that, should her husband die unexpectedly, his children theoretically could evict their stepmother.

To my friend, this state of affairs felt patently unfair. She spoke up, requesting that she not be left in the lurch. And eventually, her husband gave her the legal protection she deserved. But the process of negotiating for her rightful protection pained her, too. She felt, justifiably I believe, that her husband should have *wanted* to take care of her and not leave her unprotected. Had they discussed such issues earlier in the relationship, there would have been less opportunity for hurt and resentment later on.

What's Yours, Mine, and Ours

A second core issue to resolve before marriage involves the blending of your two families. If one or the other of you has growing children, you are marrying them as well as each other. You can avoid problems later by facing this fact now, which is something a former high school acquaintance of mine failed to do. As Casey related to me at a recent high school reunion, she remarried in midlife only to find that "her" kids and "his" kids could not get along under one roof. The unconventional solution? This married couple moved into a duplex, and they now live in adjacent separate quarters with their respective broods! Casey admits this is not an ideal living situation. She regrets having remarried without thinking through the ramifications of her decision.

Caretaking

If one or the other of you has elderly parents who require your time and attention, you are now assuming this responsibility as a team. My 52-year-old neighbor began a happy romance with a new man to whom she became engaged. Unfortunately, before the engagement, she had only limited exposure to his domineering but dependent mother, whom the son wished to have live with them. The would-be bride tried everything to make things work with

Mom, but she eventually called off the wedding when she saw that the son was incapable of rising to his wife's defense when the situation called for it. Fortunately for my neighbor, she recognized the sad reality before making a full commitment to this man.

Nesting

More often than not, couples who come together in midlife have already established households of their own before marriage. Where do you plan to live? His place? Yours? Or do you plan to acquire a neutral new living space that becomes yours together? When at all possible, choose the last option. While couples can certainly find harmony living in each other's former homes, there will be fewer conflicts, less likelihood of territorial disagreements, and a stronger vision of your collective future if you move into an environment that is new to both of you.

Of course, this option is a luxury that may not be available to you. In that case, strive to make the "old" environment a clean slate onto which the new spouse can make an imprint. Put into storage all items not needed for your current life together, thus giving maximum closet and home-office space to the new occupant. Be willing to redecorate or at least to compromise on the aesthetics of your shared living space. And by all means, remove artifacts reminiscent of a previous mate!

A final note: Learn to discern between the big issues and the small issues, and with the latter, try to be flexible wherever possible. Discuss in advance what aspects of your old lives may not be portable. A man who has hosted in his home the same cigar-smoking, Monday-night poker group for the last nine years may find that his new wife would prefer a rotating game—one that occurs on her turf every sixth week instead. Or a new husband whose business life requires that he rise at five-thirty A.M. each day may not appreciate the late-night phone calls his new wife traditionally receives from her best girlfriend. Be open to altering minor aspects of your old routine and respectful of reasonable requests for change. This does not mean sacrificing your individuality or your autonomy. And, indeed, you may find that there are a few accommodations you are not willing to make. But even when a specific request *feels* unnecessary to you, try to look at the matter from the other person's perspective. If you've married a worthy mate—which we assume you did!—the request probably has merit.

Guidelines Can Be Liberating

Stages I, II, and III of the interview process are designed to be guidelines for separating out serious prospects from men who do not fit the bill, and for determining how well matched you and a serious prospect might be. No set of guidelines will work for you if you adhere to them so slavishly that there is no room left for spontaneity or flexibility. By the same token, without a serious screening process to lead the way, you can too easily waste time and energy on unsuitable or unmarriageable men. Will using the interview approach with a new man make you uptight and self-conscious? It may feel unfamiliar at first, as would any new way of doing things. But after you get the hang of it, the interview approach will actually put you at ease. In truth, knowing that you have a fact-finding process to help you sort out information about a new man can be liberating. The guesswork is now gone from dating. You do not have to wonder about all the issues relating to this man's potential suitability, because you have the tools for finding out the right answers yourself.

As we have seen, finding a mate after age 35 challenges one to maximize not only opportunities but also time. The final chapter of this book addresses the preciousness of time and the art of appreciating and applying its higher purpose.

12

Seize the Day:
In Praise of Time

"While we're talking, precious time is fleeing:
seize the day . . . "

—Horace (Roman poet, 65 B.C.–8 B.C.), *Odes*

Life is a collection of moments, and the quality of our existence on this planet is determined by how mindfully we cherish them. Some people are so absorbed by guilt about the past, or so racked with anticipatory anxiety about the future, that the joys of the present remain unavailable to them. Such individuals do not grasp a fundamental truth: Life is not about the destination but the journey.

When you ask senior citizens to reflect on their lives and to list any regrets they might have, they tend to speak not about acts committed but rather of paths not taken—the myriad opportunities for growth and enrichment that they passed up because of fear, ignorance, distraction, or plain inertia. Have we not all said of ourselves, at one time or another, "I wish I had done that," or "Why didn't I follow up?" or "If only I had taken the chance!" These second thoughts, turned and twisted and amplified in hindsight, reflect windows of opportunity that closed on us because we neglected to act at a decisive moment—a moment of promise that may not have come our way again.

Psychoanalyst Rollo May, writing in *Man's Search for Himself*, comments on the direct relationship between an individual's willingness to grab hold of life's offerings and her feelings about the prospect of aging. The best way to face anxiety about growing older is to make sure you experience every moment to the fullest measure, says May. In other words, to echo the biblical directive introduced in Chapter One of this book, "Choose life" by striving for a proactive, appreciative involvement with the world around you. Rollo May elaborates: "Man dies like every other form of life. But he is the animal who knows it and can foresee his death. By being aware of time, he can control and use it in certain ways."

Indeed, an awareness of time is one of the qualities that distinguishes human beings from other forms of life. All cultures, from that of Papua-New Guinea to our very own, pay homage to the power of time by celebrating festivals centered around agricultural change and seasonal renewal. Thus we have the national holiday of Thanksgiving, and even regional events such as the welcome to spring celebrated in Washington, D.C., with an annual Cherry Blossom Festival. And what are rites of passage—rituals we enact to mark the movement of individuals through various stages in the life cycle—but ways of collectively recognizing time-bound milestones? A tribal ceremony in Zambia announcing a girl's arrival at puberty, a wake for a deceased relative in a village in Ireland, a wedding in a Methodist church in Texas—each of these happenings bows to the power of time.

Time Is a Gift

In his thought-provoking book *To Life!*, theologian Harold Kushner speaks of time as being not just cyclical but directional. "Every day is a brand-new day, one that has never existed before," he writes. "Today is not just another Tuesday; it is a brand-new Tuesday. This month is not just another step in the recurrent cycle of the seasons. It is a blank new page in the calendar waiting to be filled in." Seen in this context, time becomes a precious commodity, and each moment a chance to celebrate its value. There may be other moments, of course, but this very moment—this particular opportunity placed before you—will never come again.

I believe that women, as a group, grasp more than do men the fact that time is irretrievable. The explanation is biological: A woman receives a mini wake-up call every 28 days or so—an internal monthly reminder of degeneration and renewal and the inexorable march toward mortality. Nineteenth-century essayist Henry David Thoreau once observed that you cannot kill time without "injuring eternity." Women instinctively know this to be true, even if they do not always behave that way.

In matters of the heart, the woman who respects and guards time finds less reason to lament lost opportunities and unrealized dreams. That is why the sanctity of time turns out to be the core, unifying principle of all the themes outlined in this book. By accepting responsibility for her personal life, focusing on her goal, and clarifying what she is looking for in a mate, the conscientious woman acknowledges that moments are to be maximized, not squandered. Whenever she passes up a Nowhere Man, or says no to a burdensome workload at the office, or relinquishes the comfort of her routine in favor of an enriching new experience, she affirms that time is precious and must be used for a purpose that nourishes the soul. And when she decides and expects to know a man and his intentions long before beginning an intimate relationship with him, she acknowledges that time is a gift and that she wishes to use it in ways that elevate her life.

We do not need to look any further than the delicious comedies of Shakespeare to find women for whom a respect for time seems second nature. Once these "queens of comedy," as H. B. Charlton refers to them, become "conscious of their own desire, they are master-hands" at achieving it. And what they usually desire is marriage.

In *Much Ado About Nothing*, a play about courtship and the complications of wooing, the mirthful Beatrice finds her true match in the young Benedick. But Beatrice does not succumb to Benedick until she has inspired him to act swiftly to redress a wrong committed against her female cousin—a wrong that is a central plot of the play. Beatrice thus uses her favored position with Benedick as an opportunity to ensure happy romantic outcomes for everyone, including herself.

Rosalind, the warm and witty heroine of *As You Like It*, offers no less a role model of enlightened proactivity. Banished from her uncle's palace through no fault of her own, Rosalind disguises herself as a man and takes refuge in the forest where she knows her new love, Orlando, to be living. Once there, she learns that the lovesick man has been pining for her. Maintaining her male disguise, she offers herself to the young Orlando as his tutor to help cure him of his romantic affliction. Rosalind thereby orchestrates a reason to be in Orlando's constant company and to know him better. This proximity in turn leads to a favorable romantic resolution to the play.

Seizing the day yields favorable romantic outcomes in life as well as in literature. To seize the day does not suggest that a woman need be pushy, desperate, or inappropriate with men. But, to paraphrase the Lucille Ball quote that prefaced this book, it does mean that she must recognize what is an opportunity and what is not, and that she must act when opportunity presents itself. Responding to this call may require a woman to overcome her false pride, her natural shyness, or her inclination to play it safe. There is "no time like the present," wrote novelist Mary de la Riviere Manley in 1696. Three hundred years later, the observation strikes us as being thoroughly modern and on target.

It Can Happen to You

At age 42, Patricia feared there would be no marriage and children in her future. Frustrated by the seeming futility of the dating scene, she chose instead to concentrate on her career as an executive secretary to a businessman in Chicago. One of the perks of her job was the occasional use of her boss's family lakeside vacation cabin when they did not plan to occupy it. So it was that one week toward the end of summer, Pat settled in at the rustic retreat for some rest and relaxation. Living on the property were the caretakers—a married couple with whom she had become friendly over the years.

The day after Pat arrived, the caretakers received a surprise visit from a friend of theirs, John, a 34-year-old forest ranger from Wyoming. John, along with his German shepherd, was passing through the lake region on his way east and was staying at a local motel. That evening, Pat had dinner with the caretakers and John, whom she thought was not only a very nice man but also the most attractive man she had ever seen. The foursome had great fun together, and they continued to have a wonderful time together over the next three days.

When John eventually packed up his van and prepared to leave, Pat snapped some candid photographs of him with his dog. She waved good-bye as they pulled away, trying not to let her imagination run wild; after all, she warned herself, John was eight years her junior—and compared to her urban existence, he lived the life of an uncomplicated small-town guy. They were from those proverbial "different worlds." What could ever come of it, anyway?

And yet, he had been so *nice*! It was this fact that impelled her to take action a week later when the photos came back from the camera shop—John's handsome, guileless face peering out from every frame. Pat sent him a nice newsy letter, enclosing the pictures and complimenting the great poses of the dog (she couldn't very well say what was really on her mind, now could she?). Before signing off, she added that, if he ever found himself in Chicago, he should look her up—she'd be delighted to show him the sights. He wrote back. It was a sincere, beautifully written thank-you note; clearly, John had taken special care composing his response.

Pat had seized an opportunity by sending the letter and the snapshots to John. This gesture, designed to keep their interaction alive, in turn gave him the opening and encouragement to take another step: To her surprise, he called several months later to say he would be coming to Chicago and would like to take her up on her offer to be his guide. He did come, and their age and geographic differences receded as the two began discovering how much they actually had in common. John later admitted that he knew from their very first evening together that Pat was the woman for him.

After giving the decision a lot of thought, Pat eventually concluded she belonged with John. She moved to Wyoming to marry him, experiencing some predictable culture shock and a challenging period of adjustment. They have been married five years now. Workwise, she traded her urban job for a responsible but low-key position with the local chamber of commerce. What's more, she became a mother in the bargain to John's two children from a former marriage. "After all those big-city types I dated over the years," she explains, "I had finally started praying to God to just please send me a good man. And he did!" Divine intervention or not, it was the letter and photos that Pat sent to John that set the stage for all that came after. While another woman might have considered making a move, Pat actually followed through. She used the moment to its fullest potential.

An even bolder step was taken by a woman named Maggie, whose route to the altar was delineated for me by a mutual friend. I'm particularly cheered by Maggie's story because at the time of her marriage, Maggie was well into her 40s and her groom was well into his 50s. And neither of them had been previously married. So two very entrenched souls had been willing to move outside their respective comfort zones and become a couple. But I'm getting ahead of myself.

Maggie first met Richard at a Fourth of July barbecue, but they took little notice of each other at that time. Or, more precisely, Richard took little notice of Maggie.

Apparently, she had paid attention to him that day, because three or four years later she recognized him from across the room at a sales convention. Customarily shy and reserved, Maggie gave herself a little pep talk, then approached Richard as he held court in a small circle of other men. Yes, of course he remembered her, he fibbed. They chatted for a few minutes. Then Richard whipped out his business card and suggested that, once the convention ended the following week, Maggie should give him a ring. Perhaps they could get together for lunch.

Three or four weeks later, Maggie ran across Richard's business card while she was cleaning out her purse. She had found Richard intriguing; however, he had not been very gallant at the sales convention. She questioned whether his suggestion of meeting again was even sincere. But she was not dating anyone at that point in time and reasoned, in essence, what do I have to lose by calling this man?

It turned out that Richard was pleased to hear from Maggie (this time he *did* remember her), and they ended up having a leisurely lunch at a wonderful oceanside restaurant. Richard told Maggie he'd be traveling for business for the next six weeks or so, but that he'd like to see her again when he returned. And he did. Often. Richard and Maggie married one year later.

This event would not have come to pass had not Maggie seized the moment, put herself in the mildly uncomfortable position of initiating contact, and then followed up with Richard afterward—all this despite an unclear indication of "where he stood." As it happens, Richard stood on the fence, but he was open and receptive and marriageable. In their case, Richard merely needed Maggie to take the reins and give him ample room to follow her lead.

Sometimes it takes a cataclysmic occurrence to remind

us that time is precious and that moments of opportunity must be embraced. Such was the experience of Judy, my former coworker who now lives in Seattle. Judy had been friends with a couple named Marilyn and Alex for a number of years. They had met because of their mutual interest in water sports.

Judy kept up with Marilyn and Alex and saw them frequently. All this time, it was apparent to Judy that the couple had a troubled marriage; this knowledge made it doubly hard for her to ignore the undercurrent of attraction between Alex and her—an attraction that, for reasons of propriety, had never been articulated or acted upon in any way.

Much time passed. Eventually, Marilyn and Alex separated—certainly not a surprise to anyone who knew them well. Yet Judy made no move to further a romance with Alex, perhaps because she feared she might damage the friendship that was already in place. About this same time, Judy was hit by a medical whammy: a routine mammogram revealed a lump. Both Judy's grandmother and aunt had died of breast cancer. She assumed the worst as she awaited the results of the biopsy. Miraculously, the test came back negative; she did not have cancer, after all.

This brief encounter with death illustrated to Judy that time was too fleeting to waste. She sent Alex a love letter, revealing her long-withheld feelings; and he returned a letter with equally explicit sentiments. Judy and Alex now plan to marry. Perhaps they would have ended up together even without Judy's assertive gesture. But she believes otherwise, convinced that she and Alex are now a couple because she woke up to the precious nature of time and acted on it at the right moment.

We have all heard such stories of lives transformed because of a confrontation with one's own mortality. Told that he or she has a limited time to live, the individual separates the important from the trivial, paying attention to the people and things that really matter and ignoring extraneous concerns. But think how much more significant our days would be if we lived with this acute appreciation of time while we were healthy and things were going well!

In Judy's case, a specific event—a medical scare—sparked her decision to "go for it." But some women who seize the day do so simply because their instincts tell them they must. These individuals listen to their feminine intuition with a third ear—that part of themselves that we discussed in an earlier chapter as being all too often dormant in many modern women. Beth, a contemporary of mine whom I know from my grammar school days, is fortunate to have this traditional feminine listening apparatus very much intact.

Some years ago, Beth's work with computer systems took her to New York City for a four-month assignment. During this temporary job, Beth's immediate supervisor was an outgoing affable bachelor, Sam, with whom she became good friends. They came from compatible backgrounds, had many interests in common, and loved working together. They had good chemistry. From office scuttlebutt about Sam's prior relationships, and from his obvious attraction to her, Beth had no doubt that Sam was heterosexual. Yet he never ever asked her out.

Finally, the week of Beth's scheduled departure, Sam booked her for dates two nights in a row. She was certain he would finally make some sort of declaration. Well, on the final night, after a wonderful evening that had included a romantic dinner in a fancy restaurant, Beth received a brotherly peck on the cheek and Sam's promise to keep in touch. She returned to her dismantled studio apartment and cried herself to sleep.

The next morning, as her cab shot toward Kennedy Airport, Beth realized she could not get on that plane with her work incomplete. She instructed the cabdriver to turn around and drive to midtown Manhattan, where she marched into Sam's office and proceeded to tell him he was nuts to let her go. They married the following year.

Going for the Gold

Now that you have read this book and have begun to put its ideas into practice, you can distinguish between a genuine opportunity and a minefield. Yet you may question when to seize that opportunity quickly and when to hang back, gather more information, and bide your time. Not all of us have Beth's gut instincts to light the way—and even Beth's decision to confront Sam was a calculated risk. In the face of obvious opportunity, how do we gauge our behavior so that we achieve a favorable outcome?

To decide how to proceed, ask yourself a set of simple questions, remembering all the while that time is a precious commodity, worthy of respect. Using a separate sheet of paper that you have numbered from 1 to 10, respond to the following:

1: What do I stand to gain if I act now?

2: What do I stand to lose if I do not act now?

3: Will this same opportunity exist next week, next month?

4: What is the absolute worst thing that could happen if I act now?

5: What is the absolute worst thing that could happen if I delay?

6: Are the potential benefits so obvious that I would be foolish not to go for it?

7: Are my reasons for delaying based on a belief that my waiting will bring about a better result? Or is my delaying more a tactic born of my own laziness, shyness, or fear?

8: How will I feel about myself if I forgo this chance?

9: How will I feel about myself if I seize this moment?

10: Ten years from now, how would I wish to look back on this experience?

When we become responsible guardians of time and accept our obligation to honor it, we honor ourselves. By so doing, the beauty of each moment is preserved and our own potential takes wing. The results of this sanctification of time, if you will, can be felt all around us—in the depth of our relationships, in the scope of our dreams, and most fundamentally, in the meaning we derive from being alive.

❑

I hope this book has inspired you to seek a new level of fulfillment in your personal life. In every sphere of our existence, we make choices that either affirm or deny our belief in the future. We determine what matters and what does not matter to us by the things we do and the things we refuse to do. As such, we all become architects of the place in which we live.

Does the finding of a mate after age 35 require a bit of luck? Yes. Even with the best-implemented game plan for love? Sure. Is there a finite pool of eligible men from which to choose? Of course. But many people do marry after age 35. By using the tools offered in this book—tools that work!—you maximize your ability to be one of those people. And when you reach that marital goal, take pride in the fact that your initiative helped you create your own good fortune.

The danger in having resourceful options at our disposal is that we can become easily frustrated or discouraged when radical changes do not occur overnight. When this happens, we spiral away from the goal, blaming ourselves and questioning the progress we have made. Sometimes we want to give up the goal entirely rather than submit to more struggle. Trust me when I tell you—from my own experience— that this negative fallout is both natural and manageable.

A beautiful building does not take shape without some false starts, changes in direction, and second thoughts on the part of the builder. These temporary setbacks speak not to the worth of the project but to a fervent desire to get it right. At such times in our own lives, it serves us to celebrate our strengths. Oliver Wendell Holmes once remarked, "What lies behind us and what lies before us are tiny matters compared to what lies within us." When we carry this knowledge in our hearts, we soar.

A fragment of ancient wisdom holds that a baby enters the world knowing all the truths of existence. Soon an angel swoops down and taps the baby's upper lip, creating a dimple there. The angel's gesture causes the infant to forget everything it knew. Life then becomes a process of relearning all that was forgotten, of gradually remembering what the soul understood from the start. In like fashion, I hope that in writing this book I have brought some wisdom home to you—while this presentation may be fresh to you, the lessons are the old ones—truths once known but forgotten, lying deep in slumber, waiting to be roused by a kiss.

Selected Bibliography

Aiken, Lisa, Ph.D. *To Be a Jewish Woman.* Northvale, New Jersey: Jason Aronson Inc., 1992.

Appleton, William S., M.D. *Fathers & Daughters.* New York: Doubleday & Co., 1981.

Ashner, Laurie and Mitch Meyerson. *When Parents Love Too Much.* New York: William Morrow, 1990.

Bach, George, Ph.D., and Laura Torbet. *The Inner Enemy.* New York: William Morrow, 1983.

Baumeister, Roy F., Ph.D., *Escaping the Self.* New York: Basic Books/HarperCollins, 1991.

Bradshaw, John. *Healing the Shame That Binds.* Deerfield Beach, Florida: Health Communications, Inc., 1988.

Braiker, Harriet, Ph.D. *The Type E Woman.* New York: Dodd, Mead & Company, 1986.

Branden, Nathaniel. *Honoring the Self.* Los Angeles: Jeremy Tarcher, Inc., 1983.

Charlton, H.B. *Shakespearean Comedy.* New York: Barnes & Noble, 1966.

Covey, Stephen R. *The 7 Habits of Highly Effective People.* New York: Simon & Schuster, 1989.

Cowan, Connell, Ph.D., and Melvyn Kinder, Ph.D. *Smart Women/Foolish Choices.* New York: Clarkson N. Potter, 1985.

Dowling, Colette. *Perfect Women.* New York: Summit Books/ Simon & Schuster, 1988.

"An Epidemic of Obesity." *Newsweek*, 1 August 1994: 62.

Ferraro, Susan. *Sweet Talk: The Language of Love.* New York: Simon & Schuster, 1995.

Frankl, Viktor E., M.D. *Man's Search for Meaning.* Boston: Beacon Press, 1963.

Glasser, William, M.D. *Take Effective Control of Your Life.* New York: Harper & Row, 1984.

Goleman, Daniel, Ph.D. *Emotional Intelligence.* New York: Bantam: 1995

Gould, Lois. "Pornography for Women." *The New York Times Magazine*, 2 March 1975: 62.

Grant, Toni, Ph.D. *Being a Woman.* New York: Random House, 1988.

Gruen, Arno, Ph.D. *The Betrayal of the Self.* New York: Grove Press, 1988.

Heller, Rabbi Dov. *"Unlimited Pleasure Seminars,"* 1993, 1994.

Heschel, Rabbi Abraham Joshua. *The Sabbath.* New York: Farrar, Straus and Giroux, 1951.

Horney, Karen, M.D. *Neurosis and Human Growth.* New York: W.W. Norton, 1950.

James, Henry. *The Portrait of a Lady.* New York: Random House, 2nd Modern Library ed., 1983.

Kinder, Melvyn, Ph.D. *Going Nowhere Fast.* New York: Prentice Hall, 1990.

Kushner, Rabbi Harold S., *To Life!* New York: Warner Books, 1993.

Lamont, Corliss, Ph.D. *Freedom of Choice Affirmed.* New York: Continuum, 1990.

May, Rollo, M.D. *Man's Search for Himself.* New York: W.W. Norton, 1953.

Peck, M. Scott, M.D. *The Road Less Traveled.* New York: Simon & Schuster, 1978.

_____. *A World Waiting To Be Born.* New York: Bantam, 1993.

Person, Ethel Spector. *Dreams of Love and Fateful Encounters.* New York: W.W. Norton, 1988.

Polhemus, Robert M., Ph.D. *Erotic Faith.* Chicago and London: University of Chicago Press, 1990.

Porter, Katherine Anne. *Ship of Fools.* Boston: Little Brown, 1945.

Radway, Janice A. *Reading the Romance.* Chapel Hill, North Carolina: University of North Carolina Press, 1984.

Rosenblatt, Naomi H., and Joshua Horwitz. *Wrestling With Angels.* New York: Delacorte, 1995.

Sanford, Linda Tschirhart and Mary Ellen Donovan. *Women & Self-Esteem.* New York: Anchor/Doubleday, 1984.

Scarf, Maggie. *Intimate Worlds: Life Inside the Family.* New York: Random House, 1995.

Schaef, Anne Wilson and Diane Fassel. *The Addictive Organization.* New York: Harper & Row, 1988.

Schenkel, Susan. *Giving Away Success.* New York: Random House, 1991.

Sheehy, Gail. *New Passages: Mapping Your Life Across Time.* New York: Random House, 1995.

_____. *Pathfinders.* New York: William Morrow and Company, Inc., 1981.

Swisher, Kara. "Work Around the Clock." *The Washington Post,* 7 March 1994: 1 (in *Washington Business,* a magazine supplement).

Turner, Victor, ed. *Celebration: Studies in Festivity and Ritual.* Washington, D.C.: Smithsonian Institution Press, 1982.

Twerski, Rabbi Abraham J., M.D. *Self-Improvement? I'm Jewish!* New York: Shaar Press, 1995.

Viorst, Judith. *Necessary Losses.* New York: Simon & Schuster, 1986.

Wallerstein, Judith S. *The Good Marriage.* Boston: Houghton, Mifflin, 1995.

Watson, David, and Roland G. Tharp. *Self-Directed Behavior.* Monterey, California: Brooks/Cole, 1972.

"What Really Pumps You Up." *U.S. News & World Report,* 12 December 1994: 80.

Public Speaking,
Private Consultations

Helena's book is inspired by her own experience and the experiences of the hundreds of people she has consulted with on relationship issues. She frequently is a guest speaker for service organizations and corporate groups and offers one-on-one private consultations to individuals seeking to enhance their personal lives.

  If you would like to contact Helena to set up an event or to find out more about in-person or telephone consultations, please write or fax her at:

MAILING ADDRESS:
P.O. Box 3187
Manhattan Beach, CA 90266

Fax: 310–372–2045

Or visit Helena on the World Wide Web:
www.togetmarried.com